CW01666205

Souls of The Sea

Souls of The Sea

Kelly Ladell

Kelly Ladell

Cover Designer: Bookmundo

November 2024

Published Via Bookmundo

ISBN: 978940723525

This Book is dedicated to my own three, strong, independent women,

My beautiful Daughters,

Beccy, Kristy and Evie.

Each of you inspires me everyday.

'I love you like the stars above and I'll love you till I die'

Dire Straits.

Chapters:

PART 1
Allada
1628

Chapter 1- Irisa

It was dark, the dark was the nothingness and the nothingness was deep. She felt herself drawn through into its undefined edges, slowly immersing herself in the darkness, nebulous in its depth. She felt it shimmering silk-like at the edge of her vision, grasping for the spirits that hid within the heavy and oppressive darkness. She could sense their hunger to be released. They may have been lurking in the dark but they were awake and they were watching.

She rubbed her temples, releasing the tension she could feel building within her head and pulsating within her body, pounding and painful. She concentrated harder, refocused her mind and sought out the energies within the maelstrom, for the spirits she felt were vengeful.

She forced herself back into her body, breathing in deeply, harnessing the darkness, pulling it to her, merging with it, making it part of her, hauling at those desperate, hungry energies, as they became her.

She sat up, discomfited and gasped, she could feel the darkness inside of her, she could feel it trying to entice her in, willing her to give her essence to it, to become them. She wrestled with it, controlled her mind, fought it down and slowly opened her eyes.

Irisa felt dream-like, split into a thousand pieces of energy mingling together high above herself, feeling decomposed viewing herself from above, sitting within the shade of the jambackto trees, leant against their scratchy bark, giving the impression she had merely peacefully fallen asleep beneath the sage green mottled canopy, away from the searing heat.

She was not alone in her slumbering. The hazy midday heat was unbearable and the trees provided the only real shade closer to their huts, many had their siesta now rather than face the cramped, dusty heat-filled dwellings, so no one would think she was anything other than snoozing before getting ready for the work of the afternoon.

She felt her soul soar through the warm blue sky, her long russet brown tight curls flowing behind her, golden as the sunlight lit them from within, her deep nut-brown eyes wide and fearless. Irisa felt as though she were on the edge of the living and the dead, neither part of this world or the 'after'.

Fleet of foot, carrying the strength of the monstrous, she swept through the hut where Cumo was langoring and found herself staring into deeply wicked eyes.

*****

Cumo had arrived in their small village of Allada six months earlier as the rains fell hard and swift, filling the canopies with dew-drop diamonds and flooding already muddy paths. He'd arrived with a bag containing a few personal belongings; a wooden cup, cooking pots, blankets, the clothes on his back and a story of how he had travelled from his village after the sad death of his wife and child from a sweating sickness.

Irisa had felt his rotten soul from the moment he had arrived and didn't believe his story of his family's death. However the village elders had taken pity on him and after just one short meeting had welcomed him with open arms, seeing him as an asset to their small community; a young, strong male could work hard. He said he was a pumpkin farmer and could sow a crop for them on the edge of the village.

She'd felt waves of death swarming around him and instinctively sensed that he had killed someone close to him and that he'd derived pleasure from the violence and intimidation he'd metered out.

In the past few weeks he had started to reveal

more of his grotesque nature. Since he'd moved to Allada he'd been forcing himself on many of the village women and young girls and many people already wished he had never found them on that cold wet night.

It had been almost midnight when Irisa had been awoken by an unfamiliar sound, unknowing then, that as she stirred it would be the start of one of the longest nights in her life and one that would ultimately end with her using her gift from the God Durnos - God of Darkness. She sat up sleepily in her blankets, thinking she could hear a howling, was it a wild dog? Was it one of the big cats that leapt out of the jungle to pick them off one by one? She'd heard travellers sharing stories of what had happened in other villages; blood thirsty tales of bright orange and black cats, with paws as colossal as the head of a human man, dagger-like claws that left only pieces of whomever they chose as their prey.

She wrapped one of the coarse woven blankets tight around her, picked up the blazing torch and tentatively began searching the huts perimeter. She heard a soft sobbing breaking through the silence of the still night and tip-toed a little closer to the sound, mouse-like, trying not to wake Amara and her mother.

It was such a dark, murky night, Irisa could only just make out what looked like a tiny bundle of cloth by the door. Gently, she extended her leg and poked at the bundle with her bare foot, unsure of what was lurking there. She was startled as she heard a very human 'Dermal!' If able to shout 'Go away!' it was definitely not an animal.

Irisa made her way closer to the huddled bundle and realised with alarm that it was one of the younger girls from the village, bound in clothes by their front door. It took Irisa a few moments to recognise the girl as Semali, one of the young ones that helped her mother with the goats and kept an eye on the corn and beans.

She knelt down next to the tenderfoot girl. 'Semali, what are you doing here? What happened?' she whispered. Irisa could see Semali was shaking her head but would not raise it, keeping her eyes firmly cast down towards the dusty floor. 'Semali, you came here for a reason, come inside and tell us what's happened so we can help you.'

'I can't' she whimpered, 'If I tell you, you will have to tell my family and they will disown me! I didn't know what to do Irisa, I didn't know where to go. I knew I couldn't go back to my family's hut , then

I thought about you and your Neena'

Irisa didn't answer, simply opened her arms to the tenderfoot, who gathered herself within them. She held Semali gently whilst she sobbed, her eyes wide and terror stricken, her breath coming in rasps as she became more distressed. 'Shhh little one, whatever it is, you will be o.k, you're safe now, shhh.' She stroked Semali's tight black curls, trying to soothe her, fingertip strokes, featherlight touch, starting to sense Semali's body relax. As she continued to stroke Semali's hair she began to notice raised marks on her neck, she looked closer observing that they were actually deep scarlet scratches, clearly made by rough fingernails ripping through flesh. Gently she began to sing a lullaby to Semali, one sung to her as a tenderfoot. She went back to stroking Semali's hair and noticed that there was also a gap in those dense midnight curls, where a clump had been frayed clear away. Irisa felt a growing sense of unease as she tried and failed to ignore the evidence in front of her,tried to ignore the ragged tear in Semali's pretty cotton dress that was currently hanging from one shoulder and what all this might mean. 'Semali, I need you to come inside, it's only Amara and my mother and you know them don't you? We will look after you and keep you safe, please let us help.'

Slowly Semali nodded, her breathing calming, her sobbing easing whilst her tears remained streaming from her eyes. She stood and grabbed her dress tightly to herself. Just as they reached the door Hestia, Irisa's Neena, yanked it open.

'Irisa! What in the blazes are you doing? It is the middle of the night, we all need to ...' She stopped abruptly, noticing Semali, taking in her appearance and concern on her daughter's face. She swiftly formed an idea of what could have transpired, she swept back into the hut, waking Amara. 'Girl!' she bawled, shaking Amara from her dreams. 'Quickly now, warm some water and make some kirni teas for Semali'

Amara sat up and rubbed her eyes, Hestia lit a lantern. She still felt dazed and confused, was she slumbering? Was this actually happening? The sudden pinch on her arm from Hestia gave her no doubt as to that answer. Amara went to the shelves of jars, looking for the leaves they used to make calming teas with. 'What is Semali doing here? And what is going on?' Although still slumbersome, Amara could sense the urgency in Hestia's voice but was not able to work out what it could have to do with the sweet young girl that danced and sang with her sisters after their hours of toil and who helped Hestia with the crops.

Hestia took charge, wrapped a warm woven blanket over the girl, a hot cup of tea in her hands and bade her speak. As she did so, Irisa took a small piece of cloth, dipped it into a clay vessel of warm water and began to wipe the blood away from the scratches she could see on Semalis neck and body.

As the warmth of the tea and feeling of safety enveloped her, Semali began to calm, her words flowed more freely, the other women knew to give her space and silence and to let her fill it when she was ready.

'I woke in the middle of the night and needed to pass water. It was really dark and foggy when I came out of the hut and it was so hard to see. I thought I could make out something moving about outside, it made me jump at first but then I recognised the shape, it was swaying and then I heard it singing and realised it was Cumo, the newest villager, so I thought it would be fine, that he would just make his way back to his own hut.'

Irisa felt a shudder, felt her blood run as cold as her body gave way to goose pimples and fear for this young girl, this tenderfoot. She instinctively knew that her own unease about the man was about to be justified as Semali settled back to tell her tale.

'If I could have held on until the morning I would have done, I thought about running back inside but I just couldn't wait. He stunk of Mwengi, he'd vomited it all down the front of his clothes, he got really close to me and asked me what I was doing. I told him I needed to pass water and asked him to leave me alone but he just laughed at me and said he'd hold my dress and that he would keep me warm as the night was cold. I shouted at him but he wouldn't go, he got closer, this time so close the stench of him made me nauseous, he grabbed at my dress. I tried to pull away but he kept tugging at me.'

Semali paused and took a sip of tea. The woman left the silence, letting her re-group. Having a little more experience of the world than a tenderfoot, they could tell where the tale was going and however intolerable it was, however much they didn't want to hear that something sinister could have happened to their sweet Semali, they knew they had to let her tell her tale until the end in order for her soul to begin to heal and her mind to make sense of the violence and abuse forced onto her mind, body and soul.

Semali took a deep breath, put the cup down beside her, drew her knees into her chest and wrapped the blanket around her like a warm cocoon, trying to protect herself from the story she had to finish.

'He asked me if I wanted intercourse, I didn't know what that was, I didn't understand the word. He said that he would show me, that he'd shown lots of girls what it was, that he was a really good teacher and that if I was a good girl it wouldn't hurt. I tried to get back into the hut, I didn't understand what he was talking about but I knew it was something wrong because he shouldn't have been so close and when he smiled, It wasn't a real smile.' She looked imploringly at Irisa. 'Do you understand what I mean?'

Irisa nodded gently, 'yes sweet one I understand.'

'I was too scared to move then, I didn't know whether to shout for Baaba and Neena, but then I thought they might be cross with me, they might think I was being disrespectful to an elder because I wouldn't do what he asked, I was so confused.' Semali brushed her hair from her eyes and continued. 'He put his hands either side of my face, telling me to shush, he held it so tight I couldn't move it anywhere. He looked into my eyes, right into my eyes and asked if I knew what fucking was, when I said no, he was furious, said that I was lying, that I was a prick tease like all the other women he'd met, he shoved his big, fat hand over my mouth, he whispered in my ear "have you seen the goats rutting?" 'Then I understood,I knew what he was going to do to me!'

Semali wailed, huge wracking sobs that tore at the women's hearts. They knew that not a soul in the village would condone the vile behaviour of this man, but they also understood that as women they were expected to just accept rape as part of their lives, another couple of years and Semali could be raped and fucked by anyone in the village or anyone that the elders decided to give her to in marriage.

Hestia and Irisa were outraged, red-faced and struggling to hold their composure, to remain calm and quiet for Semali. Amara, always the delicate one, began silently crying, tears soaking into her coarse woollen wrap. She found a piece of clean cloth and gave it to Semali to dry her eyes, although she was so distraught she made no move to wipe her face and instead let her tears fall to the ground.

'I tried to shout, I think I screamed but I can't remember hearing anything coming out of my mouth, so maybe I imagined it. I just wanted my Neena or Baaba to hear me, to come and make him stop and leave. I was terrified of what he was going to do. He tried to pull my dress off. That's when he ripped it. I pushed against him and he fell. I tried to run away back to my hut but he grabbed me by the neck, I squealed and he slapped me really hard across the face.'

Semali quietened, smoothing her dress, feeling the edge of the hem, beautifully embroidered in bright reds and greens. She remembered making it with her mother, Neena, showing her father when she had finished, he was so proud of her for creating something so beautiful, telling her one day she would be a wonderful wife. As she continued to stroke her careful work she looked up to Irisa.

'This is my favourite dress, my family were so proud of it and now it is ruined!' Semali's tears continued to stream, dripping onto the rush floor and soaking away. She watched them as they disappeared into the grassy floor, wishing she could be washed away, cleaned by all the tears. She felt dirty, she knew what other people would think of her and it made her feel sick to her stomach.

Hestia moved to her side, frustrated at

the girl's innocence, that a dress could seem so important in light of what else the wretched man had done to her. 'Oh Semali! We can soon help to weave or embroider another for you, your dress being ruined is neither your fault or your worry, come finish your tale girl.'

Semali gazed up at Hestia and nodded. 'When my ripped dress wouldn't come off he started pulling my skirt up. I was crying "no Cuomo! This is wrong! I have not been cut and I'm not clean!" She looked wild eyed around the room, 'I have not been cut yet you see, my mother says I am not old enough yet. When I said that he laughed at me, he said I was a stupid girl who needed teaching about rutting and that he didn't care if I was a dirty whore. He slid his hands up my dress, pulled the cloth away from between my legs. I knew then that he would do whatever he wanted. He forced me to turn around and face the hut, grabbed my neck, his nails were digging in, I could feel them tearing my skin, then he kicked my legs apart.' Semali stopped, her eyes cast to the floor of the hut, shaking her head, wishing it was all just a bad dream.

Irisa urged her gently, 'Semali, tender-foot, can you be brave and tell us all?'

Semali sniffed, wiped her face on her ruined

dress and continued. 'He leant over me and pushed his thing into me, it hurt so much but he would not stop! He moved faster and faster and then he made a noise like a pig grunting and he stopped. I could feel his slime running down my legs, I fell next to the hut crying, I pulled my clothes around me and wiped myself. He told me I was filthy and should live with the pigs in the sty, that I was not a proper girl or I would not have let him do it and that I should never tell anyone, but Irisa it hurt! And I knew it was wrong, I didn't know how to tell Neena. Please help me, what have I done!'

Semali's deep black eyes implored those in the room to listen to her, to take the hurt and shame away and to hold her until she felt safe, betraying both her youth and her innocence.

Hestia, Irisa and Amara whispered late into the night around the fire, trying to think up solutions to aid the pitiful young girl. Semali slept deeply and peacefully in Hestia's bed, thanks to one of Irisa's tisanes. Irisa could hold her tongue no longer, incensed with rage at Cumos' perverted behaviour.

'We'll never get real justice! He will get away with it, he has that way about him, he can persuade others to believe what is unbelievable. I could make sure that he never does this again, he has a sickness, it won't leave him, it will fester and he will become more dangerous. You know I'm the right mother.'

' I know' agreed Hestia.'But we can't very well tell her Neena and Baaba about this without telling them about you and what power you have girl, do you really want us burnt as witches?'

'Oh Ma, of course not, but if I deal with Cumo, Semali lives without a troubled conscience and her parents are none the wiser. I know Fugra has teas and douches that can be used so a child does not occur.'

'Well if you think you need to, I think she is too young to make a child, she is only a child herself but I suppose you are right to be thorough.'

Irisa felt herself redden with anger ' Why would he do this? Why hurt a child in this way?'

Hestia sighed, 'I can't give you an answer my child, some people have cruel persuasions. They have deficiencies that we cannot understand that may make them do the things they do. I wish I could say that they do not.'

Amara had been quietly listening to the too and fro between Irisa and Hestia, she looked thoughtfully from one to the other. 'Well I know what I think' she said, wiping her eyes, red and puffy from crying throughout Semali's story. ' I think if he has done this once, he'll do it again and will it be worse next time? He has forced himself on a child! She will be classed as unclean and no man will touch her, her own parents will have to disown her.Why have that life for her when we can make a difference this time? If Irisa can use her gift we would be ridding the village of a dangerous, evil man and I don't see how that is wrong'

Hestia sighed.' We are all in agreement then. We will help Irisa so she can use her gift, we won't tell Semali's parents and we will make sure she has the right medicine to recover.'

The remaining part of the night was long and unsettled for the three women, sleeping stubbornly refusing to come despite the tiredness that bore into their bones. They all wrestled with their conscience over what was about to happen, wondering whether they would be angering the gods if they committed a god-like act and delivered justice on others.

By the time the soft pink haze of dawn light began to filter through into the hut they were tired but resigned as they spoke to Semali and outlined their plan. Rather than being scared as the women had thought she would be, Semali was still of an age where everything felt magical and she was excited that Irisa had a gift from the gods and that it could help her. She had no trouble with promising not to tell anyone about irisa's secret, she couldn't do that without revealing her own and wanted to stay in the village, marry a farmer or a fisherman and stay close to Neena and Baaba. She could only do that if everyone, including her parents believed she was clean and untouched, so she swore a blood oath and was grateful for the help of the women.

Then as though nothing had happened, it was a day like any other and they all headed out into the bright sun to start their day as usual.

Chapter 2- The Gift

For a long time Irisa had been scared to use her gift, frightened of the accusation of witchcraft. Villagers were still burned for being witches by the white people who arrived in boats, worshipping one God. They forced their way into towns and villages across the known and unknown world, professing that their christian god was the only god to worship and in his name they burnt women on wooden stakes. Irisa knew that despite the fact that many of the villagers would quickly search out wise women when their children were sick, would leave them with platitudes and prayers and marvel at the affinity they had for herbs and plants, however, she also knew that behind their backs they called them witches and did not trust them, just as they did not trust Fugra who had taught them in their small village.

That lunchtime the women enacted their plan. Irisa went and sat under the shade of the trees and began to meditate, she could feel the darkness surrounding her, holding her, she felt the coldness, the desperation and loneliness, the vengeance waiting to be metered out. She made herself concentrate, breathing deeply, gaining control.

Cumo was alone in the hut he shared with another farmer, they were all out in the fields, Cumo lazy and belligerent had said he had no need to go with them and would complete the tasks around the hut, however as soon as he was alone, he went back to his blankets and fitfully napped. He felt rather than see someone in the hut with him and jerked back in surprise, startled.

'Where the fuck do you want? Decided you can't resist my cock? Everyone wants it, did your little friend Semali tell you how good it was?' He laughed to himself, giving her a crooked smile more filled with menace than mirth.

Despite his arrogance he was nervous, she could feel it, it was emanating from him in waves. He had seen Irisa appear from nowhere, he didn't have the knowledge to comprehend the magnitude of the shadows surrounding her. This was the power of the monstrous, they could deceive as well as inflict their wrath.

Irisa returned Cumo's smile, then opened her mouth, jaw seemingly breaking. Cumo screamed, hands trying to protect his face. Unimpeded now, with her mouth impossibly agape, the darkness flowed from her, wave after wave, scolding Cumo with the intense sickly accent of rotting flesh, enveloping him while he was trying to back away from the seething cloud. But it was too late and as Irisa began to keen a high pitched whine, the creatures within her left her and found Cumo.

She clutched her chest, her heart beating impossibly fast, startled as the force that came from her. She felt no remorse as she heard the screams from Cumo, the growls, the hungry mouths, the ripping and devouring. His screams for mercy began to fade away as the darkness filled the room, pouring into his lungs, his heart and then it was gone and so was Cuomo.

She had made him feel terrified, that he was nothing, just as he had done with Semali and all the other women he had tortured. Sighing deeply, she smiled and closed her eyes.

*****

She felt a jolt as her essence returned to her body, slowly she opened her eyes, relieved to find herself still under the dappled shade of the jambakto trees where she had first sat. She yawned, taking in deep breaths of clean, hot air, scented with deep red hibiscus blossoms, the smell of spice and herbs wafting from Fugras' home as twilight turned to black blanketed sky mottled with stars. She stood, straightened her tunic and made her way back to the women huddling around the cooking pot they shared.

'Hey, sit down Irisa' whispered Amara ' We saved some stew for you, Fugra made it, it's goodIrisa smiled at her friend, 'thank you, I'm suddenly feeling quite empty.'

Amara placed her hand on Irisa's thigh, they shared a discreet smile and nothing more was said.

Chapter 3- Vengeance

Amara had known Irisa since they were tenderfoots, growing up in the lush green valley by the coast of Africa. She lived in the tiny village of Allada, a hard working community consisting mainly of farmers of brazil nuts, watermelons, pumpkins, beans and some fisherman who had boats at the nearest cove.

Amara and Irisa worked together gathering herbs for the bent-backed medicine woman, Fugra. She had taken care to teach them how to identify every herb, flower, root, plant and bark that was safe to use and would give the best effect for one condition or another, how to soak them in oils or crush them into powders or pastes and how much was needed to cure and not to kill. The villagers now relied on them for their knowledge and skill of herbs, how they could blend them together to make healing teas, pastes and poultices and how their skills and magicks kept them safe and would cure them of most ills.

At times it felt like a thankless task, especially when others their age had finished their farming chores and were chanting, singing, dancing by the fire whilst they were still helping Fugra gather plants and herbs that she insisted could only be collected by the full moon or they would not be as potent, or they were helping her to prepare sacrifices to the gods, another duty they had to perform as wise women. They would then eventually stagger exhausted and empty to their flat, hard beds, late into the night, where they would still be expected to rise from if a woman needed them for a birthing.

Amara was the only one who knew of the darkness in her friend. At first she had laughed, Irisa had struggled to explain the darkness and the monstrous spirits she could sense within her, how it could leave her and enter another. She'd thought Irisa had been listening to too many of the folktales often told on a cold night, huddled around the fire, blankets wrapped around their cotton slips, many talking late into the night until the velvet blue sky of twilight turned to the russet and pink silk of dawn. She knew Irisa loved to listen, learn and remember.

Amara knew how hard home life had been for Irisa and her mother, Hestia. She knew Irisa's father was an unpleasant man, quick to anger and even quicker to raise his fist. Irisa often tried to protect her mother which meant that she was often the target for Dumas's blows. So when Irisa told Amara that she was going to try and use the god gift to rid them of Dumas, she understood the wish but could still not even begin to believe that Irisa could actually achieve what she was promising she would do to her father.

Irisa however, could take no more of her mother being black and blue, now that he had started to beat her as well, she was afraid he'd soon want more than that.

Amara had cried at the thought of all the hurt and pain that Irisa and her mother had suffered at the hands of Dumas and had thought that was why Irisa had started to talk about ending people with darkness. Amara believed in Irisa's cunning, she believed a true gift had been given to her from the gods, she believed in the wise women, in the tales from the village elders but struggled to comprehend how her beautiful, frail looking friend could control evil spirits hidden within a darkness.

One night as the moon cast its luminescence over a small clearing by Hestia and Dumas's hut, Irisa and Amara had sat chatting, laying amongst the fragrant lemongrass, staring up at the glittering stars.

Amara I can't take this anymore, last night my father came to my bed thinking mother was asleep, he got into my blankets, tried to lift my shift, mother woke and he said he was soothing me from a bad dream. I know she didn't believe him, but nothing else was said, tonight I am going to end him.'

Irisa was very calm, resigned to what needed to happen. She'd thought long and hard about what she had to do, she knew he would kill her mother if they told anyone what he had been doing to them. Irisa was still considered too young to be cut then, too young for Fugra to cut her to make her clean and respected ready for a husband. If the village knew she had been touched by a man, she would have to leave, ostracised for something she had no control over.

She'd tried to talk to her mother, trying to convince her to run away, to try and get to another village, taking the fishing boat with them and getting to the next cove, but her mother was resigned to the fact that wherever they went, Dumas would find them, she feared he would never let go of something he viewed of as his property.

Irisa turned to Amara, smiling, ' Stay with me, see what happens please?'

So Amara swore that whatever happened she would stay with her friend. She rested her head on Irisa's shoulder and waited. She felt Irisas's body tense, neck bent back, mouth agape and widening grotesquely, eyes rolling back in her head, then she watched as Irisa's eyes filled with a blackness, she could feel herself being drawn into the shimmering within the dark. She jerked away frightened but when she looked back all she could see was her life-long friend Irisa doing something dangerous to try and save herself, her mother and others from yet another man who wanted to hurt and control them. She suddenly felt a great compassion for Irisa and what she had been going through and remembered her vow. Whatever was happening, this was her friend, her family and she would not abandon her, so she calmed herself, rested her head against Irisa and waited.

They sat peacefully for some time, the fire burning down, Irisa stiff as the standing stones at the edge of their village. Suddenly Irisa gasped and fell backwards, Amara held her head in her lap until she came to.

Irisa's father had never been seen after that night and no-one could find a reason why but he was not a well liked man, with his quick temper and selfish ways and he was soon forgotten, especially by her mother who moved about the home with a new sense of purpose, growing crops on a small patch of earth outside of their hut,which she bartered for cloth to make clothes for her and her daughter, freed from a life of pain and anger.

Hestia told Irisa that she had been asleep, that she knew nothing of what happened but smiled at Irisa as she said it. She then spread a story throughout Allada and the nearby villages that he had never returned after going to the cove to check on his fishing boat. It was a journey of less than a mile but everyone knew how dangerous the deep cove and the tides that ravaged it were, so no one asked questions. The villagers were happy that Hestia had still got the boat and could make a living from fishing for the bright silverfish that darted throughout the ocean and formed the main part of the villagers diet.

Iris had tried to talk to her mother about it afterwards but her mother had told her not to tell a soul, that it was their secret, that it was god given and not to be scared of it. She was just glad that her father Dumas was gone, her mother making a living and that there was a calmness in the house that they'd never had before, so she listened to her mother and told no one except Amara.

Soon after, Fugra, the wisewoman had taken both her and Amara on as apprentices. One afternoon as the sun melted in a puddle of russet and orange into the horizon, Fugra had asked Irisa to stay and gather centrellus- a herb they gathered at sunset and sunrise, that they then made into a sticky paste that helped to heal open wounds, fought infection and saved lives, so Irisa had not refused such an important task. As they gathered the herbs together, Fugra stared at Irisa intently, muttering an incantation as she did so, so deeply that Irisa had begun to feel uncomfortable, sensing the crone's gaze upon her.

'Look at me child'

Irisa stopped and glanced back to the crone. 'Have I done something wrong, Fugra? I am trying to learn the incantations as well, I just get so muddled with some of the words' She put her head down waiting for Fugra to chastise her.

'Child, I know there is a world in you, a power, a strength and a darkness' Fugra paused and Irisa flinched and started to move away.

'No! You have me wrong. I don't understand what you speak of!' She knew as she spoke that her heightened voice and speed of speech would not be convincing Fugra of her innocence, she was terrified of what she would say.

'You misunderstand me child, I am not scared of this power, I'm not branding you a witch, but this power is all encompassing and you will need someone to guide you through how to use it. I know you have used it before but I can teach you to look into that darkness, to harness the power that dwells within it and how to make sure no innocent is hurt by it, including you.' Fugra continued to gather herbs as though she had not spoken of something so full of magic. Irisa was unsure of how to respond, so took Fugras' lead and continued to gather centrellus and did not speak on it for the rest of the night.

Irisa had known there was no point in arguing with Fugra she seemed to see and sense all, and so was not afraid when one night Fuhra called for her, bade her drink devils claw tea, sat crossed legged, looking into the fire, thinking of the darkness. Irisa had become curious about her power but it also frightened her, so she gave her trust to Fugra and accepted her help with an open heart and a sense of relief.

She began to reminisce of all the times she and Amara had been called out to the sick or the dying and learnt how to help them from Fugra's instruction. Irisa came back to herself from her daydreaming, feeling the sting of a hot wooden spoon on her back. Fugra was bringing her out of the darkness.

'Why do you not listen to me! If you do not stay strong and stop the damn daydreaming, they will bring you into them, you'll become one of the monstrous and you will leave this earth! What use will that be? Durinos, our own god of darkness gave you this skill, have respect and use it well! I need you to find every evil spirit that hides in there, one by one, take control, then you will be able to bring justice to those who mean us harm, you can protect us more than any army the Elders can put in place.'

'Some are not evil' Irisa stated quietly.

"Of course they are girl," hissed Fugra ' They are just manipulating you.'

'No!' Irisa shouted, ' There are some who are hurt, angry, guilty and their anger is the power I sense, but not all the spirits are evil, some have unjustly become spirits, that's why I can easily use them to seek out vengeance for us, I am using them, let us not forget that, it is not a purely innocent thing I wield, whether a gift from Durnos or not.'

*****

Irisa's body sunk to the earthen floor, they had been practising for hours, as soon as she felt herself slip away, she could hear them all, whispering, seducing, caressing and she found it harder and harder to resist their calls.

'Please let me rest, Fugra, can we not try again tomorrow, please?'

Fugra gave a sharp nod, choosing not to answer Irisa's anger. 'Mmm, I suppose child but as soon as dusk hits, I want you here at my hut with or without Amara.'

Irisa nodded her head in agreement, grabbed Amara's arm and together they ran off to her mother's hut.

Chapter 4- Control

Hestia came to the door rubbing her eyes, trying to shake off the pull of the dream that had held her hostage for most of the night, memories of desperately explaining to suspicious elders who did not trust women in any situation, where Dumas had gone, why he had just disappeared from the village and uncomfortable memories of most of the villagers talking in hushed whispers as she passed them as they got on with the days tasks, trying to protect Irisa from the gossip, trying to hide her own fright that her daughter may have to face the elders for practising witchcraft at some point in her life.

The dream had left her with a heavy heart and a flutter of confusion and anxiety for her daughter which tumbled out as anger towards the girls and she felt unable to control it.

'Must she keep you so damned late? Come in the pair of you, you'll freeze to death out there without blankets! Get into the bed I've made for both near the fire, I'll bring you a pot of fish stew, you must be famished! If she is going to make you stay so long she needs to feed you! Stupid old Crone!'

Hestia went to the pot and filled bowls using a ladle, the stew, thick with corn, beans and fish. The warm, moist smell wafted through the hut and Hestia finally smiled knowing that at least the girls would have full bellies while they slept.

Hestia had used the fast swimming lean silvery fish- Sardinillas, that swam in huge silver shoals off the coast, glinting and glistening through the clear sea as the sun shone through the azure blue coastline, knowing it was a favourite of Irisa's. It had always comforted her as a child and she knew that after spending all her energy and emotions learning her craft with Fugra that she would need something to warm her inside.

Hestia came close to her daughter,'Praise Durnos for your gift but can you truly do this Irisa? Can you control them? There have been others before you, spoken of in legends, but they went mad with terror and lost themselves, I am afraid for you my love.'

Irisa snuggled into the warm, fleshy arms of her mother inhaling her scent of soap and fish.

' I believe I can, Mother.' she said with a truth that she felt in her heart. 'It is hard, I am fighting but I do believe I can make Durnos proud and use the gift as he meant me to. Fugra is tough but she only wants me to be safe and to learn the monstrous and their ways.'

'I hear it's a confusing realm to find yourself in, they say in the legends that it is like they are all woven together in there, like when we weave cloth for our tunics I suppose.'

'Weaving, weaving,' mumbled Irisa. 'She smiled at her mother and Amara, ' Right tomorrow I'll try something new.'

It wasn't long before the girls were curled together, blankets wrapped tightly around them. They stayed by the fire until dawn stretched its pale yellow sky across the horizon and flooded the hut with light and gentle warmth.

*****

The day started early but Fugra, knowing that she wanted Irisa back that night let the girls go home and have a sleep in the hot midday sun. Irisa made her way up to the rocky outcrops to a stream, where white willow and jasmine hung close to the water, the scent of musk and flowers filling her body with a sense of light and calm as she drifted off into a gentle sleep.

Irisa!' She felt herself being shaken and jolted awake.

'Come on Irisa, it's been dusk for nearly an hour, Fugra will be mad.'

The girls ran together giggling, their hair and tunics flowing behind them as they made their way down the stream, back into the village and to Fugras tiny hut in the woods.

As they drew near, they could see that Fugra was pacing up and down and muttering to herself. ' There you are! Come on we can wait no longer, the crescent moon is rising, I believe this is the time for Durnos to lead you into the darkness.'

'I've had an idea too, Fugra, of how to pick one of the monstrous at a time, I ...'

'No time! Just do it, if I see you struggling I will bring you back, now come into the hut this time, I want you to lay on the blankets by the fire and think of the darkness, we will all say a prayer to Durnos to guide you well tonight, remember you have the power over them do not be deceived by their devil tongues, listen to the god who owns them.'

Irisa walked into the small hut, Amara dragging slightly behind, clutching her hand tightly, she could feel Amara startle at the sight in front of her.

Irisa squeezed her hand for reassurance and pulled her inside. A tang of copper hung heavily in the air where Fugra had sacrificed an owl to Durnos, a night bird to a night god. She had laid the feathers over the blanket and made Irisa lay down amongst them.

Fugra moved to the corner of the hut and returned with a small rabbit, tied by the legs so it could not escape.

Amara looked questioningly at Fugra, ‘Why have you got a rabbit in here? You need not make another sacrifice! Is it not bad enough that you have already killed such a beautiful creature?’

Amara felt a great affinity with the animals and wildlife in their village and could not bear the thought it would anger the gods who protected them, bringing bad luck upon the whole tribe.

Fugra sighed, ‘Girl, if you are going to be here to help your friend, then help, no point being all weak and sobbing. Irisa calls the darkness into her, once it is she has to pass it to another, if not it will destroy her, I felt a dumb rabbit better than one of our dumb villagers.’

Amara took the animal from Fugras arms. ‘ I understand but it is cruel to make innocent creatures suffer.’ Amara stroked the soft fur of the buck and felt it stiff with fear at her touch. ‘ Please give him a swift end, Irisa, be as kind as you can.’

Irisa held out her hand to Amara,’Of course, I don’t like their suffering anymore than you do but if I can control this gift, it may save our lives one day.'

Amara nodded, 'Travel well my friend, I'll be waiting for you.'

Fugra leant over Irisa, ' Chew leaf, it will aid your journey.'

Irisa did not know what the leaf was that Fugra gave her but it was bitter and thick and made her feel dizzy, just as when she had drunk too much mead wine at a festival. She took a deep breath and reached out. She asked Durnos to guide her to the monstrous, she remembered what her mother said about being woven together, thick coarse threads making woollen tunics. She imagined that each of the monstrous had its own weft and this was what she had to find and pluck if she wanted to gather different spirits, she would be able to weave a new pattern with the deathly threads. Initially she had been met with resistance in the dark cold place, they tried to confuse her, to hide or to dominate. She kept her strength, Durnos brought her clarity and she held onto her love for Fugra, Amara and her mother to keep the balance of light and dark.

Irisa could faintly see a thread, spider web-like, sticky, cloying yet beautifully delicate, lace-like. She reached for it and heard a hiss of defiance and knew she had won. Soon after she pulled at another and another, this time she brought herself back, she poured the darkness and the monstrous she had brought through into the rabbit, caught and trapped to sacrifice to Durnos, showing him the power she had gained and the control she had mastered. She sat up and slit the animal's throat.

Fugra was waiting with a pot of rooibos tea to refresh Irisa's body and mind. She shared with Fugra what had happened and for once Fugra looked content. 'Good, maybe now you can use this power and not kill the rest of us at the same time.' She was smiling as she said it though and that meant she was pleased.

*****

It had taken two full years to learn what dwelt within that space and how to call it forward at will. She never used it to hurt the innocent, she called on the darkness to rid the village of the foulest and sickest among them and all the while, only herself, Fugra, Amara and her mother knew and understood the power she had or fought to control.

It didn't always result in a death or ending someone, she had learnt control, calm and peace when she entered the darkness and when needed she could now find an essence that would terrify a person into ceasing their sadistic ways or their sick pleasures, without them being devoured by the blackness. Those terrified but not taken, were never the same afterwards but never harmed another after the monstrous had visited them.

Instead Irisa used her gift rarely, instead, focussing on helping others with the medicinal remedies and healing the sick and injured along with Amara and Fugra and she felt at peace. She often looked back on that time of discovery and wondered what her life would have become if she had not learnt to use her power or had chosen to reject it, although she knew she could not. It was as much a part of her as Amara's thick glossy curls were part of her.

Allada gave them a simple life but they were happy.

Part 2-

1630-
The Raiders

Chapter 5- Nzinga

One bright hot morning as the girls made their way to Fugras hut they overheard a group of elders talking anxiously and stopped to hear what they were gossiping about. News had begun to spread along the coast, village to village that raiders were coming , that they had desecrated sacred places until no magicks remained, that Una, Earth mother, was angry and shook the ground. They were sure the gods were angered, tempestuous storms raged over the valleys and the sea foamed and hissed as the waves broke across the craggy cliffs, but it did not stop the raiders, they worshipped other gods and they laughed when they heard the villagers trying to warn them.

The elders prayed hard and ordered every villager to do the same, to save them from the white faced men with wild, violent and sadistic ways and only one god. The elders believed that in praying to the gods for fierce weather, many would be killed before they got out of their boats. So, the villagers prayed unceasingly, day and night and yet still the raiders were coming and the villagers began to fear what their future held and questioned if they had a future at all.

The village had started to feel eerie, there was a sense of foreboding so strong you could pluck it from the air. There was a sense of fear but also of resignation, they knew the raiders would come, they knew they would take many of them as slaves, kill any that got in the way but they knew not when this would happen. Many fashioned weapons from whatever they could find. It was a village of peaceful farmers and fishermen, so weapons were scarce, the fisherwomen had knives that they used to gut the fish and they held them close morning and night, the farmers fashioned weapons from their simple utensils and kept them in their huts at night ready to protect the sick, elderly and vulnerable and their precious children.

It was early one morning before the sun had risen, still a soft apricot shimmer close to the horizon, when a cry went out that people were approaching. Everyone that could gather weapons did so, this was a village of equals, of women who had been warriors in their earlier days and they stood alongside their men now, proud to be fighting for a greater good.

As the small group of people entered the village, walking tightly together, they first noticed that they were not the white faced marauders, these were tribesmen! Rich tribesmen. The group dismantled, revealing that in their midst was their Queen, Queen Nzinga, with spear and shield held aloft to reveal herself, the mighty Nzinga, accompanied by her war council - her sisters, Cabu and Fugil.

Those who were nearest fell to their knees, hands out in supplication. Nzinga was a fierce warrior Queen and much respected among her people. Those further back could hear gasps and silence that had suddenly engulfed the village, slowly coming to understand who was amongst them.

Queen Nzinga stood, tall and imposing, lean with a full lipped smile and wide open eyes. Her red and green cloak swathed around her, held with a magnificent gold clasp to match the golden crown she wore upon her head, glistening in the half lit dawn. The villagers were mesmerised that this all powerful leader had deigned to come to speak to them and they were full of grace and gratefulness, they would soon be bitterly disappointed.

Fugra pulled Irisa and Amara to the front of the crowd as they gathered around their leader, eager to hear her speak.

With a loud, clear voice, Nzinga addressed the village. ' My people! We are peaceful farmers of the

earth and sea but we are also brave fierce warriors. We have long fought the raiders and their stealing of our people for their own gluttonous means. It is with a heavy heart I tell you that to ensure they do not take all of us, I have had to agree terms with them.'
There was a pregnant pause and the villagers did not rush to fill it, they could not believe the words she was using, this warrior Queen who was ready with a huge force to war with any tribes that tried to take them or their land over.

'I have agreed to send those of you that would have been punished for crimes, those of you who myself and my advisers feel would cause the outsiders to raid us regardless of the terms I have agreed. For those of you women that have skills with herbs and magicks, you will be sent away to avoid calls that we are a nation of witches, if that label stays we will have no one left to trade with. It is a sacrifice, but one we must pay, may our gods protect you. Those of you that can leave and find safety, do so now, there will not be another chance. The raiders await my return to the coast, I shall meet with the Portuguese governor and the captain of the ship they have sent, once I am there, they move on to the village.'

A Stunned silence filled the space where they

usually gathered for rituals and festivals, a space usually filled with laughter, music and souls lifted and joined in joy. Not so today, there were stunned faces, looking to one another, silently seeking an answer to the questions that filled their heads. Many of the kings and Queens had had their heads turned by the goods the merchants with their ships brought, stopping at Africa to trade, barter and to gather slaves, Queen Nzinga was no different.

Despite being a proud warrior Queen, when the Imbargalas came to her with spices that made her mouth water, cloth, so fine it was translucent and felt like wearing mist on a summer's day, clothes so soft, they caressed the skin - not like the coarse woollen garments of her own country. Jewels from deep within the earth, that sparkled like night stars in the sunshine, she took it. She wanted it all, every single jewel. She had heard the tales of the Kings and Queens of the Portuguese and English courts and wanted to be seen as the equal she was.

Nzinga had known she would have to make an alliance with the Portuguese in order to save her people from the yearly summer raids by the slave ships that came to wrench families apart. Her sisters - Cabu and Fugil, her war advisors had been adamant that this was the only way forward, the only way to have some control over their people and country, but still the concessions had left her with a heavy heart and uncomfortable. She would still have chosen to fight the marauders, although she knew that risked the lives of many more than if the alliance she'd created could hold.

Whispers began at the edges of the crowd, people having let the Queens' words sink into their hearts and minds began to realise what her words meant, Fugra could not contain her ire, she turned and spat on the floor, hissing.

'Irisa, what can this mean? Our Great Queen in league with the evil we seek to fight!How can this be happening? Has she turned her face from the gods? You do know she means us, she is talking about wise women, the very people that are sent to her and her family when they are sick or one of them has a baby stuck in her belly, oh then we reign supreme, we are blessed and virtuous, but she'll send us away to those damned marauders, who worship a god who believes burning us to death is a good thing, that it will purify our souls. What shit is this?'

'Fugra, please be quiet, someone will hear, we can not argue our fate, we know that, there must be a reason she is willing to send us away. The gods must have willed it.'

'Listen to yourself Irisa, you know there is so much more to the world than just the one we all know and talk about, she has been sucked in by fancy clothes and jewels, look at her garments, how is she able to be a warrior in a grand bloody cloak!'

Fugra moved forward, onto her knees, head to the ground, Irisa tried to move her away, Fugra slapped her hand in anger. The Queen's protector moved forwards, pointing his spear at Fugra's head. ' Go back to your hut Crone or you will find this spear through your guts, you disrespectful whore!'

'Hold that spear Now!' Nzinga's voice cut through the air like a knife, the protector moved back, sullen faced and angered.

'Speak wisewoman, I would listen to your counsel.'

Fugra lifted her head but stayed on her knees, her arms towards Nzinga, imploring her to listen.

'My Great Queen, warrior heart, bravest of souls, I implore you to reconsider this act. You are sending your own people away, you know what we will have to face once we are slaves to them, you know we face death or worse, please fight! Fight as your brother and father would have fought.'

Nzinga smiled at Fugra and bade her stand, gesturing for her to come closer. Fugra kissed her hand, wishing her the health of the gods, slowly making her way beside Nzinga, Queen and Crone together.

Nzinga held Fugras' hand aloft, ' This crone is the bravest amongst you! You may be farmers and fishermen, weavers and workers but you all have weapons, you know how to fight an enemy, you have done this before!'

Her anger shone through the clearing, touching them all, many bowed their heads in shame for letting Fugra be the one to voice the villagers distaste at the suggestions of the Queen.

'This is always the way! You men who have told others of your warrior adventures but never had to bury a child, toil the ground till your hands bled, given birth in a heat hazed field. You know nothing of courage, look upon this woman! She knows as a wise woman she will be taken by slavers, do you think she will go willingly, even though as her Queen I have ordered it? No she will not! I would rather feel the teeth of a thousand wild dogs than let another take me and my freedom and despite the alliance I have agreed I expect you to do the same!'

Nzinga's voice levelled now, softer, trying to reconcile with her people 'I did not choose to do this on a mere whim, we are being punished by raiders from along the coast, along with other tribes from the interior, we can not fight them all. I have gained this alliance in order for them to agree to help us fight the tribes that pursue us, so we can remain free, those of us who can survive'

'I am your Queen and I will have your respect and compliance, this is the will of the gods and the burden of our people, although I pray one day it will not be so. Now go! Prepare as best as you can, they will not want the old or the sick, you will be safe. Try and hide the children if you can. Those who are taken, go with the love of your Queen.'

With that the war council and the servants gathered around their Queen and together they left the village as surreptitiously as they had entered it.

Chapter 6- The Juniper

Off the coast of Africa, Carlos de Vasconcelous, owner of the mighty merchant and slave ship 'The Juniper' waited. He had commanded his Imbargalas to set up camp in readiness for when the slaves from Allada were brought to him and he could gauge his earnings.

He gave a sneer as he held the brand of the the ship in his hand, knowing that within the next short weeks, he'd be placing it into a blazing fire and pressing it firmly into the flesh of each of the dirty savages he was taking across to the Americas with him in his cargo hold, naming them as his property.

He was proud of his dealings with the Native Queen, the warrior Queen they called her, bitch, to him she was no more than any other commodity, just like any other slave, sold and used all over the globe. It stuck in his craw that he had had to give her the ceremony and respect that she had demanded. How could she be his equal? Did she really expect to be treated as royalty? He had conceded purely because he had negotiated a deal that ensured he came away with maximum profit for as little trouble as could be managed. It would be difficult to separate the man from the merchant, he had been doing this for so long now even though he no longer knew what sort of a man he was. He was getting slaves for free, without the usual accompanying battles that they had had with all savages when they tried to take them, which inevitably led to the loss of some of his crew. If bowing and scraping to a bloody savage woman ensured this didn't happen, well, so be it.

Many of the slave masters or owners that he supplied, worked their slaves to death and continuously needed them to be replaced, who else would do all the filthiest and degrading of jobs?

They needed more to replace those killed through ill use, little food and water and no sleep, so had started to gather seafarers and cross the dangerous seas to replace their workforce. They took strong young men to row their huge ships, they took the women and the girls as slaves and concubines and they took without mercy. Putting up a fight ensured you were stoned to death and there were no gods to help you survive.

They gathered the stolen into groups, women tied together with ropes, herded together like the goats that roamed the higher ground, men in wooden yokes, two together, one in front of the other. They were forced to trudge through the valley, over the cliffs to their ships where they held them below deck like rats until the sea journey to the New Americas was complete.

Carlos enjoyed that part, the voyage. He could have everything- the freedom of the sea, the company of a slave that he could keep for himself, one that would gratify all of the sexual thoughts he could muster and do it without complaint - not like the English whores he's tried. Of course he would have to allow his Captain, ship's surgeon and first mate a slave as well, that just meant he'd have to take extra at Allada, he refused to be out of pocket by one guinea. This part he did not enjoy- waiting, waiting for the return of his men. He hadn't gone with the raiders to gather the slaves, he sent his first mate and a group of Imbargalas, sailors and soldiers, whilst he awaited them with impatience, which he took out on his men.

Chapter 7- Deals

Vasconcelous knew the villagers of Allada were doomed, that they'd been sold into slavery by their own Queen, he found it highly amusing of course, that they had no knowledge of this or why this might happen, this was the way that Nzinga had wanted it, so there was no time for rebellion. She had promised him that her people would go willingly, under her instruction, those that had been carefully picked for either committing crimes or being a danger to the village.

He remembered when he had first met Nzinga it had been a blazing hot afternoon, the golden sun golden and gleaming, searing down onto skin and bone. Nzinga had agreed to an audience with Vasconcelos, he'd sent word to her that he was gathering slaves to take to the New Americas for plantations, to work in the fields or the big houses and that he hoped they could agree terms that left them both a little wealthier and happier.

Nzinga was a fierce Queen and led her people well but even she was not oblivious to the benefits of selling those who had or would cause trouble or upset. Last time Vasconcelos had come, he was on his way back from the Arabic countries where he had traded slaves for spices and cloth unlike any she had seen or felt before. She remembered with a sense of shame how deeply she had been drawn into the prospect of material wealth. He had laid a piece of silk across the floor in front of her and lifted it for her hands to touch, caressing the material, reminding her of the colourful sunsets and the light misty mornings, so light was it. Then he had put sparkling, hard, glassy gems in her hand, sapphires of the deepest blue, rubies of fire filled red and emeralds as green as the sea. Every jewel glittering in the sun akin to the stars at night and she coveted them.

Vasconcelos had brought out a necklace made of the richest of green emeralds, which he placed around her neck. As he slid the gold and emerald choker on, she felt startled by the coldness of the shiny metal and the stones that were contained within it. She had felt a pride, knowing that she was wearing the jewels fit for a Queen of Nations and not just villages and her heart became greedy for more. Vasconcelos had promised a shipment of spices, fabrics and jewels in return for slaves. She had been happy to discover that she could get rid of any vipers in her nest without guilt. Of course until the last moment, when she had felt burdened with the task of giving the villagers some notice of what might become them, until then they obeyed her rules and paid their respect and dues. The villagers of Allada had always felt safe when they heard that raiders were coming, they had faith in their gods and the Queen.

Nzinga sat on a chair in the hut, laid thick with hides, soft and comfortable for one so important whilst her visitors had to sit on the floor beneath her, ensuring she could always look down on them with the disdain of a leader.

Vasconcelos bounded in with four of his men at arms and a mariner whom he introduced as the Captain of the Juniper.

'Talk, men of the sea, what terms do you offer to me? How many slaves will you want?Show me what delights you bring to our humble land'

Vasconcelos stood straight and proud, he understood he had to deal with these dark skinned savages to get the slaves he needed but he felt a disgust that this fucking woman sitting on a chair made of wood, wearing a cotton fucking dress thought she was a Queen just because she had a few people under her! How could this be a Queen? She was nothing more than a black savage who ate better food than those who served her and had a hut a little bigger. He smiled, gathered his thoughts and began to outline his agreement.

Chapter 8- Stolen.

Amara had cried a soul's weight in tears by the time they had tried to desolate the village. Those too slow, too frail or too scared to leave the village had been torn from friends, family members and could not bear the sense of loss.

They had been gathering herbs when they were cruelly captured by the Imbargalas who surged through the bushes, a wave of angry, white men hollering a language that sounded familiar, they had been raided by the Portuguese before and some of the sounds they used had not been forgotten.

Irisa watched in horror as a broad chested man appeared behind Fugra, tall as a Jambakto tree, slippery as a snake, he grabbed her roughly by the waist, swiftly bringing a knife to her throat in threat.

'Don't move bitch!'

Fugra struggled, kicking and lashing out but the slaver had her hands behind her now, using rope to bind them.

'Fugra!'

Irisa started to run to the old woman whom she loved as deeply as her mother, Amara tried to pull them back.

'No Irisa, they'll kill us all!'

Irisa had no intention of not trying to save her, she stood up as tall and proud as she dared and shouted, 'Leave her you pig!' She picked up a loose rock, all she could find close to hand and hurled it with all her might towards the slaver. It hit him square in the temple, the force making him stumble and he let out a cuss towards her.

'What the fuck! You'll pay for that you Christ hating whore!'

Dragging Fugra behind him, he began to stride his way towards both her and Amara. Irisa bent to find another rock, stick, anything that could be used to stop him, she didn't see one of the other imbargalas silently making his way out of the bushes, she turned suddenly at the noise and he hit her hard about the head with the butt of his gun, knocking her to the ground. The slaver loomed over her greedily, examining her like a bird of prey with a prize, Amara next to her sobbing.

'Oi! Goncalo look! This one is worth a pretty penny! She'll be ripe for plucking! Don't fancy your chances with that one though!'

They started laughing then, letting off steam the only way they knew how, deprecating women, making themselves feel masculine and empowered, unaware that this was the opposite of how they appeared to everyone else.

Fugra had stopped resisting the moment that she had seen Irisa hurt, knowing it was the only way to stop them, she had no wish to excite them to the point where they would forget they were gathering slaves, condone their own base instincts and perhaps begin to torture, rape or murder them.

'Let's just get them back to the fucking village, the quicker we're back on that ship the better.'

'Just because you don't want to fuck the old whore! You can have a go at these two if you like? Which one shall we fuck first?' He chuckled to himself, full of pride for capturing beautiful healthy women, they'd be making money alright and when they got to the plantation they'd be making it with their legs wide open and their mouths shut!

Irisa felt sick, they talked of rape so inconsequentially , the raiders clearly thought of them as nothing, as not human. She took a deep breath and readied herself for the torment ahead, taking Amaras hand and whispering,

'Whatever they do, bear it, they will not win your spirit!'

But the torment did not come, not yet and not that. Instead she smelt the delicate scent of herbs as they were crushed beneath trampling feet, the rasping of cloth against bushes and more of the Imbargalas appeared.

'Gonzalvo! Stephano! Stop this now! What in the name of the good lord are you doing? How can I teach these natives to come to Christ if this is how you treat them? Vasconcelos assured me that this would not happen upon the Juniper and it will not happen on this part of the journey either!'

Both men put down their knives, shame faced, flushed cheeks, reddened skin already burnt by the intense heat. The man slowly approached Fugra, untied her hands, gesturing for her to move towards Irisa and Amara, which she did as quickly as her legs could carry her, her feet oblivious to the sharp roots that cut them as she ran. They held each other, sweating with the heat and trepidation, clinging to the hope that their gods had blessed them, that they would survive this. He moved closer towards the three women who were cowering low to the ground, huddled together tightly. Irisa noticed his strange clothing. The other imbargalas were dressed in rough linen shirts, ankle length trousers, this man wore a long black robe with a large silver cross around his neck. He bent down to them and spoke in halting Alladian,

'I apologise for the men, they do not always follow the laws of their betters or their Christ. I am Francisco, Father Francisco, I am a priest, I believe you say Nganga? I have travelled with the ship, I am here to bring you to the one true Lord, Jesus Christ and mind your spiritual welfare on this journey.' He held his hand out to the pair 'Do not be afraid, we will walk together.'

The women looked at one another, they could all sense that there was no harm in the man, although they did not understand his beliefs and had no intention of changing theirs, they did all however understand that to accept this man's kindness would stand them in good stead for the journey ahead of them. He helped Irisa and Amara to their feet and put out a hand to Fugra who ignored him completely, preferring to struggle to her feet alone, she would give this man nothing.

'Come, follow me, we are all gathering in the village centre.'

Fugra, livid and nervous in equal measure followed, muttering ' Al Kahir! We have no choice! Why does he make it sound like a shitting glorious journey rather than what is really happening here!'

Chapter 9- Terror.

The group were huddled together and quickly reached the centre of the village, where only a short time ago, their Queen had come to warn them of this exact scenario.

'Well, voiced Fugra, We have fought as hard as we dare, now we must go with the love of our Queen and the will of the gods as she bade us do.'

Their hearts fell as they saw dozens of their tribe, knives, guns, sticks at their throats being jostled into groups of men, women and children. They were herded towards the small group of women, the terror emanating from them in waves. Some were with children, some on the border of womanhood, some still children crying and clinging to the legs or the tunics of their mothers and sisters who were too scared themselves to be able to offer them any succour. Many of the sick and elderly had stayed where they were as the Queen had guided them, many more tried to hide their children, bade them go off into the forests and to stay there until they could no longer hear sounds from the village. However, despite the promises of their Queen, when the Imbargalas came through, they killed any who were too sick or injured to take, they had no wish to risk them surviving whatever damn jungle fever they had and joining another tribe ready to fight against them when they raided again, people with grudges were dangerous.

As the slavers rampaged through the village on that searingly hot afternoon, capturing those who tried to escape, including Semali, whom they had tied with ropes to two other women, hauling the string of women and men between them, Irisa noted that they had been badly beaten, the captured were unceremoniously discarded to the village centre, one of the white bastards shouting at them:

'This is what happens when you run away! You have bought you ignorant bastards! You will come with us or we will beat you to death, is this understood?'

Many had looked away, Irisa noticed that within the writhing group that one of the farmers wives was heavy with child, she was trying to stem the blood from a lengthy open gash close to her eye, struggling as her hands were tied to another woman who could not aid her, she was an elderly woman and in a stupor from fright.

Irisa shouted 'Magra! Magra! Are you and the

baby well?'

Magra nodded her head gently but Irisa could see with her own eyes what had been done to this innocent.

She gestured to the slaver' Let me help her, please let me help her!' She nudged her way towards the group and to Magra. She was so focussed on the woman that she did not see the slaver coming closer, she heard Fugra scream her name, then felt a deep pain in her stomach as the raider kicked her hard with his leather boots.

'Fuck off bitch! She ran away, she is ours, we'll do what we like to her, let me show you what happens when you interfere.'

Irisa could hear herself screeching, 'no!'

But she could not react in time. The raider, after a sideways glance at Irisa, swiftly kicked Magra in the stomach with his heavy boots. Magra fell to the ground clutching her stomach, sobbing.

Irisa was crying, shouting 'Magra I'm so sorry! Magra!' Fugra and Amara grabbed her away to the side of a hut, pulling on the rope to gain some small amount of freedom. Fugra held Irisa in her arms,

'Now child this is not the way to help, we must do what they say, at least for now. Listen to me child, we need to survive, we need you to use your gift when we are our lowest, trust me Irisa, this is not it! No more rescuing, we'll have plenty of time for that.'Irisa calmed, sitting with Amara until she could control her breathing and savage temper that burnt beneath her skin at the thought of the torture these men would inflict without mercy or conscience.

Fugra made her way towards the men as they readied the slaves for the next part of the journey. They had originally pushed her away, Fugra had clung to the girls, pleading with the savage to let them go. Her voice fell on deaf ears, the slavers spoke mainly Portuguese with the odd Arabic or Afrikan word or two, learnt from years of voyages to steal slaves from all over Africa. Words yes, however speech flew over their heads and they did not want to learn the language of what they saw to be dirty slaves and their prisoners.

It had been Amara with her gentle voice and her simple hand gestures to indicate that all three of them were medicine women that had persuaded the mariner to accept Fugra, explaining how she could keep them all well. That would always be useful on a ship and if the dirty slaves could look after themselves the less he'd have to do on the journey.

After the beating, many of the Alladians became subservient and left without a fight, although it gave Irisa some consolation to see several of the slavers had cuts, scratches or black eyes where they had been fought against.

*****

The sunlight fell upon every atom it met, turning it red, burnt, raw. There was little vegetation this close to the coast, the earth was sandy and difficult to cultivate. The only hope of shade was to find a group of Jambakto trees with their thick, waxy, sharp edged leaves, deep green with bright yellow veins pulsing through them.

Irisa felt every grain of rock filled dirt and sand as it pulled through her feet and toes as she was dragged across the ground, roughly handled by the mariners. She clung to Fugra and Amara, frightened that if she let go she would never see them again. They were exhausted, they had been walking for days, with little food and water. She looked skyward, praying for Gynos to bring a storm so dark they would not be able to leave the coast, maybe she would have enough time to get the three of them away so they could hide until the raiders left.

The bright incessant sun blistered down to her

neck, her whole body swathed in sweat, her coarse tunic now in rags, clung to her body, rasping slowly against her skin as she moved. She pushed her hand up to her forehead to shade the glaring sun from her eyes as it sparkled like glittering jewels in the night.

As she dragged her exhausted feet and aching body through the searing heat, her mind drifted away from the dusty ground and back to Allada, she and Amara gathering herbs for Fugra, pulling the short spiky leaves off the rooibos trees as they made a refreshing tea for colicky babies. Irisa felt herself relaxing back onto the coarse bark of the trees, smiling at her friend Amara, waving as she came to sit by the fire and chat. She felt herself spinning, releasing, darkness was at the edge of her sight, it started to crowd her eyes.

'Irisa! Irisa! Oh Aleaziz! My friend, please, get up before they see you or they will kill you'

Irisa slowly opened her eyes, sat up, touching tears as they flowed down her face,
Dripping into the parched sand. She knew now she was not back at Allada and remembered what had happened as it all came rushing back to her, her chest gave a thump of horror.

'Oh no, Did I go away into the darkness, Amara,

what have I done?'

Fugra moved closer, her voice a whisper on the soft breeze, ' Calm yourself my child, you are exhausted, we all are, you merely fainted, no darkness was released, you have enough strength to save that for the moment when it is the only thing that can be done.'

Amara was beside herself with worry for her friend, 'Irisa please get up, that pig slave gatherer is coming, he will leave you here injured or kill you if he thinks you're weak.'

Irisa sighed, 'Amara calm yourself, we are all weak, we are exhausted, even the Imbargalas, look at them.'

Amara risked a glance at the imbargalas who had gathered by the few shaded trees that edged the cliffs lining the shore. They were sun raw, blistered, their pale faces not used to the heat and she could see that they were struggling with bloodied feet and weary looks.

Irisa slowly started to move. Pero, the fattest of the mariners approached with a swagger and a smirk. He was one of the few that had long leather boots to protect his feet from the harsh ground and they thumped as he moved closer to the group of women.

'What the fuck is going on bitch!' he glared at the three women, poking each one hard in the chest as he spoke, 'You think we have time for village fucking gossip! I suppose you're making plans to kill us, I know what you are, witches! Evil!' He made the sign of the cross before them, seemingly to ward off evil. 'Walk now or you will be left to die in this god forsaken heat!'

He slapped Irisa hard across the face, she felt her lip splitting and the blood soak into the sand, she let it drip, trickling down her lip and onto her tunic, she made no move to wipe the blood away and turned to face Pero directly into his eyes, letting him know that his violence did not scare her, she had felt worse from her own father, this alqarf, was nothing.

She held onto her thoughts, her power, if it came now would be seen by all, they'd see what she really was and think her a witch. It was a dangerous time for the people accused of such things, as well as their families, they were not just killed but burnt alive to purify their souls, she knew she would have to bide her time. She didn't even flinch when he went to slap her again, he stopped in front of her face, his knuckles grazing the tip of her nose. Irisa put her hand on his and held his wrist without speaking, hoping he could see some of the power she held buried deep within her own eyes.

Pero stopped, muttering to himself 'fucking witch, why the hell are we here! I fucking hate this place and I bet we don't even see any profit from these mangy slaves!' He kicked the dirt with his boots, glancing downwards quickly as another slaver stamped over.

'Pero stop! What are you doing? For the love of god leave these slaves alone! They are supposed to be salable when we get back to the ship on the other side!'

Pero returned his gaze to his filthy boots, 'They are gossiping about us' he mumbled, 'They plan to kill us in our sleep, and these three- he pointed as he shouted- they're fucking witches, I'm sure!'

'Don't be so fucking stupid Pero! The men are in yokes! What are the women going to do? This one looks exhausted - he pointed to Irisa- We all are! Now move away before I give you what you gave her!'

Pero did move away, though stubbornly dragging his heels, muttering 'slave lover' under his breath.

Aleixo chose to ignore the remark, he knew Pero too well, since childhood and he knew Pero hated anyone with dark skin, he just wished he didn't act like a petulant child all the time.

Part 3-
Aleixo and Pero

Chapter 10- portugal

As children Aleixo and Pero had lived in the small fishing village of Nossa Senhora de Luz in Portugal. There everyone knew one another, worked together, helped one another, life had been hard but good.

It was a small community, a group of hard working fishermen who went out daily in their small boats, sometimes, not far from the shore, catching sardines, then the villagers worked together to bring in the catch, smoke some, clean some, sell some or barter for goods they couldn't produce like crops. The soil near the sandy coast held no nutrients, it was a difficult place to grow corn or maize.

Aleixo and Pero were often sent together to the shore line to find any of the fish that had been dropped, it all helped the pot of fish stew go further. If they were really lucky and there had been a good catch, they were allowed to gather what they could find, light a fire and roast the little silvery fish until they were crisp and delicious, eating them in swift bites, laughing together, making up tales of what they would do when they were fishermen and how they would catch bigger than these little sprats.

Their days were filled with dashing across the hot damp sand, like lizards, hoping from one foot to another, the sand so hot it burnt the soles of their feet, then they would dive into the shimmering water, so clear they could see the bottom, the tiny fish grazing against the amber glow of the thick sand.

Sadly this simple but blissful existence didn't last forever. Just as in later life they would rip others from their homes and their homelands, villages along the Portuguese coast were raided by the Moors every summer. Villagers stolen away as slaves for plantations in the new countries of the South Americas.

As children they had witnessed more death and destruction than young eyes should ever see.

One warm summer evening, the sun had begun to fade gently away, melting into the ocean, a slight breeze blowing across the sand and cliffs, taking the edge off of the heat of the day. Children were still playing outside as their parents worked, an evening like any other.

It had been Pero that had heard the first cry from the village,

'Raiders! Raiders coming!'

They had been helping the fishermen on shore as they prepared their boats for sailing the following day at sea, mending the nets was a job for small agile fingers, reworking the threads so the tiny fish couldn't escape. The fit and young amongst them were gathering weapons, trying to prepare a defence, knowing they could not protect the whole coast and that somewhere and somehow these savages were coming to take whatever they could.

The women were gathering the children together, some screaming, some so calm they appeared dazed, stupefied, parents so terrified their children were pulling at their clothes begging to be picked up, wanting their elders to make the terror and the uncertainty stop, but they could not react.

They could not understand why their village was always amongst the raids in the summer, they were fishermen, there was no gold, no treasure here. True they did trade in spices along the old trade routes but the merchants who made the money did not live in the poor villages but in the big houses further inland in the start of the bigger settlements.

But come they did, and when there were no riches, they took people. Selling slaves was a lucrative business and the Moors were no exception in taking advantage of finding people to overpower, manipulate and sell.

Some of the villagers refused to leave their small wooden homes or their tiny stone dwellings, simple homes but everything they needed was within them and they were adamant that no barbary slavery was going to take that away from them, they believed they would be safe if they could bar their doors and be silent. It didn't save them, as the marauders clambered through the village searching, always searching for potential slaves, leaving blood and bodies behind them from those who fought, those who would have been able to get to the next village, warn others and gather support were all butchered. The marauders, filthy, blood soaked and savage.

Even the spaces under beds or tables or hidden nooks above attics with straw were not secure enough. Most were dragged out of their hiding places, throats slit if they didn't comply.

News did spread village to village and they knew that the years of good weather and calm seas had brought more Moors and more raids. They came and took the strongest of the youth in villages up and down the coast as slaves for themselves and to sell.

Those that had enough warning did manage to

escape and had sought sanctuary in the nearby stone church, Igreja da Misericórdia - Church of Mercy. It was inhabited by roman catholic monks who served the community. As well as spiritual guidance, they worked the land and fed the poor. Many of the monks accompanied crusades or voyages to gather slaves with the hope of 'rescuing the souls of the savages' and to bring them to god.

Lay Brother Francesco da Silver was close to taking his holy orders to become a priest. He had always been a quiet and contemplative child, always thinking of others. His family had been so proud and not entirely surprised when he announced his decision to join the church. His mother had at first tried to persuade him to think again, he was her only son and she wanted him to have the joy of fatherhood, the love of a woman and the warmth of a family, however after months of trying to persuade him otherwise he assured her that he had the love of a family and would have the love of god and that that would be sufficient to see him through his life within the church.

Francisco had herded many of the women and children into the church, the entrance had been barricaded. Thankfully whatever evil ran through the veins of the Moors, Francesco and his fellow brothers were grateful that they observed the sanctity of the church and did not attack it.

When the Moors had gone it had been Francisco that had gone with distressed survivors to clear up the blood and detritus left behind by these savages, trying to get back a semblance of normality. It has stained his soul seeing all that violence and blood, he vowed he would do all he could to convert as many souls to his one true god as was possible in his mortal lifetime, hoping this would bring peace.

Pero had wandered around the village, a small boy of only eight, lost amongst the horror of what had once been his happy home. He'd tried not to look at the dead, their eyes skyward, their mouths agape, huge gashes across their throats, or their insides falling out from blood drenched rips in their stomachs.

The smell was unbearable, coppery, strong, sickly and it pervaded everything. He'd been hiding with his mother Ana and his sister Beatriz, older than him, she had originally been trying to hide him in her skirts where he'd run from the beach where he'd been with Aleixo.

His mother had held him gently by the

shoulder.

'Pero, listen to Mamma, I need you to run and run as fast as you can to the hill caves, do you understand?'

They were all crying now and Pero started sobbing uncontrollably, snot dripping down his face along with his salty tears.

'No Mamma! I will stay with you and Beatriz, please Mamma.'

Beatriz held tight to her mothers skirts, gently crying and held her brother close.

'Pero, please, you must go, see if you can find Papa, save yourself, there is no hope for mamma and me, we'll either be taken or worse but you can get away, you can be free from these animals, please my brother, I beg you!'

He looked at his mother whose eyes were glistening from the tears she held within them, trying not to let Pero see the terror she had for her and for her children.

'Go Pero, Go!'

He took one last look back as he ran from the back door, he hid himself under the sheep straw in the back pen and kept an eye out for his mother and his sister. For many years after that moment, Pero wished he had left as his mother and sister had bade him do, as an adult he understood that his mother and sister knew exactly what would happen to them and that they were trying to protect him from embarrassment and shame.

Pero risked moving closer to the open back door as he began to hear a cacophony of sound erupt from there. Suddenly he felt himself being dragged, feet scraping roughly against the sand and rocks and brought back into his home. His mother and sister were fighting two other men. He could see that one had removed his trousers and was moving his mammas skirts. Pero knew he didn't want to see this and turned his head. It was immediately yanked and turned towards his mother and sister again, the marauders grip making him dizzy and faint.

The Moor leaned into Pero and whispered - 'You will watch you tiny maggot!'

Despite all the wriggling and struggling, he was forced to watch as the men shoved themselves up and under his mothers' skirts. She made no noise, faced the ceiling, kept herself calm, knowing that fighting them would give them more pleasure. When all three had finished raping her, they turned to Beatriz.

'No!' Screamed Ana, 'Please not my daughter,

she is not yet of age, I beg you!'

The Moors laughed at her and grabbed Beatriz by the arm and threw her down on the floor. One fumbled with her skirts, whilst another fumbled with his trousers.

'Turn her over, I will fuck her like their pigs fuck.'

He leaned his head over Beatriz's, she could smell the spices that had been used in his head dress and tried to pull it off. He slapped her hands.

' Oh no, Now we have to tie you, don't struggle bitch!'

Beatriz was frantically trying to wriggle free, calling out, screaming for her mother, 'Oh god help me, help me mamma!'

Ana could not, she was bleeding profusely and quickly losing consciousness. The most comforting thing she could offer her daughter was whispering, ' I am here daughter, I am here, it's all o.k.'

Beatriz screamed as one of the men entered her, shoving his cock into her hard, this was power and not sex, he wanted to control and hurt her. She began to sob as a second man came over and shoved his cock up her back passage. As the men thrusted faster and harder into her, she sent up prayers to god that she would still be delivered to heaven as a virgin, feeling a deep shame, although she did not choose this, this was not the love whispered about between women and young girls as they did the laundry or made the food, this was violence and rape and she could not stop it.

Pero watched in horror, tears streaming down his face, guilt filling his heart that he could not stop this as his mother left this earth and his sister suffered, the Marauders having left as soon as they'd wiped the dribble off their trousers.

'Mamma No!'

Beatriz was brought round by the sound of her brother's voice, she turned her head gently, looking him in the eye, 'Go now Pero, go, I will always be with you in your heart, with our mamma.'

Chapter 11- Survival

Pero ran then and ran without looking back, he scrambled towards the caverns in the North and on finding one of the largest, where sometimes the sheep were kept in bad weather, he made his way in and to the back of the cave. He sat there with his head in his hands, sobbing, covered in scratches from the climb, his body aching from the exertion, his mind racing with what he had seen but could not work out. He stood up and screamed into the cave, howling with grief, like the wolves they sometimes heard on a summer evening.

There was a rustling at the back if the cave, Pero prepared himself for another Moor to come out to kill him but it was not a Moor that greeted him but his own father, who came out sobbing,

'My Son! My Pero! Forgive me, my son, I am a coward. I saw their ships coming into the harbour, I knew what it meant and yet I stayed here and did nothing, forgive me.'

Pero was small and needed reassurance, he threw himself into his fathers' arms sobbing.

'Mamma and Beatriz, Pappa, they hurt them, they did things to them and hurt them, then they killed them. Beatriz gave herself to save me and told me to run. I did go back, I promise, I promise I went back but one of their savages caught me, grabbed my neck and made me watch while they did things to them. I tried to turn away, I tried.'

His last words were muffled and lost amongst his wracking sobs, his father stroking his hair, bidding him be calm and that all was ok, the whole time knowing it could never be ok, he had fled and left his son to face what he should have born and now it would never be the same.

Holding tightly to his fathers' hand, together they stayed the night in the cave, only after many hours when they were sure they were safe did they start a very small fire and huddle together closely for warmth.

'Try to rest pero my boy, tomorrow we will have to go back to the village, we have to be brave and strong to do that. You are going to see bodies and death again, but I promise you my son, I will do all I can to make sure you never see it again.' He held his son tightly, trying to squeeze away his own anguish and doubt about whether he himself would be able to face the village and the horrors it held in the morning light.

*****

Pero sat up in the damp, dark cave. He had squeezed his body against his fathers for warmth, their tiny fire long expired. He heard a scratching sound, was that whispering he heard? He nudged his father awake.

'Pappa, I think they have come to kill us, I can hear something.'

Rest easy Pero my boy, it is probably rats or birds, they are awake in the night, we however need to sleep, tomorrow is going to be a hard day.'

His father rolled over, quickly settling back into an exhausted sleep. Pero still thought he could hear whispering, he stayed sitting up, they would not surprise him this time. He scrambled around with his hands in the dark until he found some loose rocks, he grabbed one and held it tight in his palm. He heard the noise again, this time, without thinking, he hurled the rock towards the source of the sound.

'Ouch! What the!'

Pero startled, 'Aleixo?' Could it be his friend that he heard or was he dreaming. This time he whispered a little louder, 'Aleixo?'

He waited for a reply and just as he was giving up he heard, 'Pero! Pero!'

This time his father sat up, there was a faint

light coming towards them, it grew as it got closer, and then there in front of him, like a mirage was Aleixo.

Behind him, cautiously and slowly moving were his mother, two sisters and a younger brother.

Pero and Aleixo held each other tightly.

'Ah Pero you survived, thank god! I don't know how many of us there are left.'

'Not many,' replied Peros father. 'Denaris, is that you?Come, sit on my coat, I'll make us a fire, I think we are safe enough now.'

Denaris nodded, 'Thankyou Pedro, I will help, there is wood to gather.'

Denaris was a strong independent woman, having been a widow for many years and having to bring up a young family, she was not used to others doing things for her and found it hard to accept help when it was offered. Today however when Pedro said - ' Rest, I'll watch the children.' she had nodded her assent and sat down, physically and emotionally drained now that she knew the attack had passed and that she still had her children with her alive. She could not summon the energy to do anything else,

Once the fire had been lit and the children were sleeping fitfully, Pedro and Denaris shared how they had survived, spoke of the horrors they had witnessed and whom they knew would have to be buried tomorrow.

Pero and Aleixo may have survived the slave raid but they never recovered from the horrendous attack and the images of walking back into the village together the following morning. The pools of blood and mutilated bodies haunted their dreams their entire lives.

Pero remembered terror and blood most nights in his dreams, they were always violent and red as he remembered the blood soaked limp bodies of his mother and sister and the joyful cries of the Moor marauder as he held his crescent knife high in the air in triumph. Pero was bitter, his hate turned inwards, tainting his heart and soul and he became a cruel and vengeful man.

Aleixo had always forgiven him his faults, understanding the struggle between dark and light that raged within him. Life had gone back to as normal as it could in Nossa Senhora Da Luz, relatively quickly the dead had been buried with prayers from the monks sent up to the gods for all the tortured souls.

The ones who had been left behind tried to return to life, stoically completing the day to day chores that life insisted be completed and so they made it through childhood to adolescence, friends like family united through a shared horror and grief.

Pero and Aleixo shared a small fishing boat they had made together after the Moors had left. They fished every day for the small sardines that swarmed their warm waters, watching their slim, shimmering bodies trying to escape their nets, despite all their childhood brags of catching bigger and bigger fish than their elders.

Pero resented this existence. He saw others, like the Moors, who had come in fancy clothes, better boats, fabrics, bangles. Even those he visited to barter with inland seemed to have better homes, more food and warmer clothing, drank mead, owned horses, he however saw he had nothing, that it had all been taken from him by the Moors and he was bitter at the thought that he did not even have the same.

Peros' hate turned towards his fellow man, woman, anyone else who was as black as the Moors. He could blame his loss and the poverty he felt he should not have to endure, believing he deserved more, why would God not reward him for surviving? The only one who escaped his wrath was Aleixo, his faithful childhood friend whom he loved like a brother, although at times he couldn't help but be resentful towards Aleixos' purity and kindness, which he felt could smother him, however he stayed loyal to Aleixo.

Pero survived because he only had to feed himself and his father. Aleixo, on the other hand, struggled to bring fish and bread to the table for his family. With two sisters, a mother and a young brother, he knew that if he did not do more, this winter when the bitter northern winds came in and the ice and snow returned, they would all freeze to death and starve. His mother Denaris, a fierce and loving matriarch had sworn that it would not happen, that she would go into servitude or sell herself as a prostitute and be proud of it if it fed her family but Aleixo knew he would never let that happen and would do anything to ensure it didn't.

When the Barbary slavers had arrived at their coast asking for young, fit men to join their raids for gold and slaves, Pero had been quick to sign up; he'd persuaded Aleixo to do the same. Aleixo had signed up with reluctance, he didn't like the idea of the raiding and violence that had blighted his own childhood and in his heart he had no wish to go to another land and to do the same to others but he could see no other way to provide for his family and his village would grow rich on his earnings when he returned.

The Barberys were wealthy and they paid their crews well, higher than they could earn or barter in many years. This way his family would deal well with every winter and summer afterwards and have a fire to sit by, God would have to deal with his conscience and his guilt when he reached his death day, until then, he had to keep his family alive and would do what he must.

Pero loved the idea of wealth but it was the thought of having power over the slaves, of dark skinned slaves that really excited him, made his blood boil and fester. He would now have a chance to avenge his mother and sister, he would slowly rape and kill their women just as the Moors had done to his.

At the same time in the town's dusty church, Francesco had also agreed to go with the Barberys. He felt in his heart that this was God telling him to go and spread the word to the world and begin to bring peace to it.

Part 4-
The Journey

Chapter 12- The Trek

Pero's hatred seethed within him but he knew he would bide his time to get the satisfaction of revenge. He knew once they were on The Juniper, they would herd the slaves together like cattle and who would miss one or two cattle from such a very big herd.

'Right, that's it, we break here before heading down the cliffs, Pero go and see to the men, they need water.'

Aleixo loved Pero but he took the responsibility of being a slave hand seriously, he wanted them to be healthy and well when they reached the port and Vasconcelos saw them. He knew what he had been promised and he would have his men examine every single one of those slaves to make sure he was not short changed.

He approached the three women who were trying to comfort one another, the older one was putting some sort of salve onto the split lip of the slave girl that Pero assaulted, he felt drawn to her, she had the darkest eyes and hair he had ever seen, so dark they reminded him of the black-blue shimmer of ravens wings. With her high cheekbones and full lips, he was mesmerised.

'I apologise for Pero, he is too anxious to get back home, he's not much of a gentleman, he shouldn't have hit you though, I hope it heals well.'

He looked directly at Irisa, who gave a thin smile despite herself,

'Thank you, I will be, this will help heal my lip,' she pointed to the sticky paste her friend had applied. 'Is it far now? Is it far to your ships? To your lands? Where are we being taken?.'

Fugra gently placed her hand on Irisas' arm, a gesture to say 'enough child' she felt no fear talking with this slaver and could not smell the same rot and evil that she had smelt drift off of the other one they called Pero.

"We now have to trek around the cliffs, until it is safe to scale them to reach the shore below, then we will board the ship, it's a mighty ship called the Juniper.'

'And then?' questioned Irisa, desperate to know the fate that awaited them all.

'Let's not worry about that yet, we need to worry about getting to the ship first, I can't tell you more, I'm sorry.'

He turned away and from under his belt

produced a large wineskin, Irisia recognised it, they used them back home, made from the finest deer skin. In Allada it would be full of fresh, clear water from the cool bubbling stream at the top of the cliffs, the Portuguese however filled theirs with rich sticky wine, red as blood, sharp with berries.

'Here, take some, this will help your lip too.' he smiled at Irisa and put the wineskin to her swollen mouth.

Thick sticky mead filled her mouth and swam down her throat, warming her stomach and she felt the pain ease. 'Please may my friends sip this too? We are so weak, I beg you.'

She looked deeply into the eyes of the slaver, he did not dress the same as the ones they called Barbary, who were savage and cruel. His floppy golden brown hair flopped onto his soft skinned face, his hazel green eyes glittering in the reflections of the sun. His soul did not fit with those around him, she found him curious and contradictory.

He nodded, 'Quickly though, I have to get us moving.'

He passed the skin to Amara and Fugra who greedily drank down the mead and returned it to him with a nod of gratitude.

Fugra touched his hand, 'I think you are on the wrong side of things young one, I sense a goodness in you that is not for these vile Imbargalas, think hard before you make decisions you'll regret, look to the light in you, what is your name?'
He smiled at the old crone, he'd never captured slaves and wasn't expecting them to ask him personal questions, he thought her quite mad but harmless, they'd only brought her with them when they noted her skill with herbs and plants, it would be good to have a healer on board the ship.
'My name is Aleixo and I thank you for seeing me, crone.'
Fugra gave a slight nod and waved him away with her hand, seemingly dismissing a slave from her own presence.

Aleixo shook himself as if skipping out of a dream-like trance, he had to stop himself from smiling at them all in return, he liked these women although he knew he should not, they were only slaves after all, a commodity he could make use of to ensure that his own family survived. He had been uncomfortable with the idea of gathering slaves from the beginning. He'd been through that trauma himself and could not find it in his heart to hurt them just because they had been taken from another land, yet he couldn't afford to look weak in front of the other imbargalas and Vasconcelos, they were experienced slavers and to them, slaves were just a product, a crop, monetary objects, but still he would not hurt them unless he had to. The raping and the torturing, so he'd been told, was just part of the experience, however he was adamant that this would not happen under his watch and that's all he could promise himself, he had to think about his family back home and what he was actually doing all this for.

'Ok men, let's get everyone up, we walk the path along the cliff edges tomorrow, it will be a hard day. Tonight we camp, tomorrow we trek.'

*****

The cliffs were renowned for their danger, they loomed tall, sharp, craggy and ominous. Large prominent outcrops lining most of the coast, huge stone fortresses guarding the lands within. It was beautiful in its rawness as well as being imposing and almost possible to scale or descend.

There were few foot or hand holds in the dark grey granite and there was no visible path to follow. Some of the slavers were nervous; they had heard tales of the lamigyers, vast white birds sent by the savage gods who would try to dislodge anyone brave enough to mount those cliffs. The villagers knew that these were not mythical beasts sent by their gods and that it was simply because they had nests in those craggy cliffs that they would attack and would protect their eggs and young to the death, but they didn't tell the slavers that, instead they let them feel a degree of terror and uncertainty for a while.

They had little option as to how far they trekked, the cliffs were too treacherous to descend at this point, they simply could not be scaled, instead they had to follow the cliff path until they reached a safe place for all to make it to the shore. Aleixo knew that the sailors had been waiting for their return since they departed the ship and left for the interior, they would be impatient to be off land again. The water folk never liked being on one piece of land for long, to them it was a place of bad spirits and bad luck, however he had to consider the best way in order to get to the ships with as many live salable slaves as possible - minimal loss of produce, hence they were walking the cliff path.

The barbary sailors had a life of wandering and sometimes loneliness, although many water folk had small family ships which they would moor alongside one another to winter, to provide a safe place from the grey winter seas and thick ice. They were a hardy people and could survive long, treacherous sea voyages which was why they made good slave traders and sailors. They had sailed these waters many times and knew where to avoid, where to take advantage of the wind so they could speed along the top of the ocean like a stone skimming a pond, but they were impatient and would create mutiny and set sail if the crew were not back as planned.

The people of Allada knew of slavers, heard of what others did but felt they had no need for them. The village worked together as one family and they all completed their roles within it, no one person had more or less than another, so jealousy and greed had no place in their lives, they were content. They thanked their gods for what they had and prayed to them when they needed help, which always came. Now that they were taken themselves, they knew what would happen when they reached the next mainland. A few of the older people in the village, Irisa's mother being one of them, had been a slave before on cotton or cane plantations, sometimes as house slaves to the wealthy landowners. They had heard tales of how they were used and they were in no hurry to become the next batch of ‘cattle fodder’ exploited for whatever perverted purposes and cruel uses the landowners could summon up.

Irisa knew that as a slave to the land dwelling on the other side of the vast ocean, they would see vast dwellings and huge fields of sugar cane,that, unless lucky enough to be used as a house slave, she knew that they would all be cloistered together in small huts with little room. She’d heard tales of buildings made of stone and wood, reaching up into the sky and that the rich had rooms of their own. She knew she had to hold hope in her heart but accept that she would now have no ownership over her mind, body or soul and would not be permitted to show emotions, thoughts or ideas. The landowners, the British and American in this new world believed that slaves who indulged in emotions were devil possessed that their hearts and heads would be overtaken by demons and they would use that magic on their owners. For all the power, wealth and privilege they professed to, Irisa and her people thought them naive and stupid. However the one strength they wielded over those in this new world, was the white folks fear of their magicks and they were quite prepared to use that.

Before the village, Irisa's mother Hestia had been born into slavery, her mother had been a slave on a huge plantation owned by a mainlander. She'd been raped by her master who denied it when she'd tried to tell him. He said someone else had raped his slave and he turned his back. Hestia had been broken-hearted and had truly believed this man's lies when he told her he loved her and would take care of her. When she lost her tiny baby boy in the fields, born before he was due, she had buried him and prayed for him, told the Master, but he didn't care, he was glad the rotten thing was out of her, lust had been his intention and not love or god forbid half-breed offspring.

Irisa's mother had said she was better off without a man in her life, that she needed no one but herself and the gods. Despite this, soon after her mother had met Dumas, guided by her family to marry 'one of her own kind' she agreed and looked forward to starting a happy life. In the plantation she had bravely threatened her Master with witchcraft and the lily- livered bully had agreed to free her and her new husband, who had not lowered himself to the violence and degradation of his family at this point. The Plantation Master, fearing his reputation would be tainted if people found out he had stuck his precious prick into a slave, eventually let them go, telling others that they had escaped and good riddance to them.

They had made their way back to Allada, where they had lived in relative happiness until one fearsome fishing trip out to sea when Irisa was six or seven, her father had never been the same after the terror of that experience, he babbled about devils and gods, getting drunk on thin beer and mead. That's when things really changed, he had been haunted by his thoughts and started to beat her mother senseless.

Hestia had often spoken about the plantation, the long, long hours in the sugar cane fields, picking up canes that the men in front had scythed. Back breaking, sweaty work and no matter how often she prayed to the gods, it had never got easier. They finished work at sunset and she would watch those sunsets in the East with pleasure, the oranges and yellows melting together like the gods had madea painting just for her. The sun rises were equally beautiful but she feared them, she feared the glorious light as it flooded the hut she slept in, glimmering like a golden veil, but beautiful sunrises promised working until your soul was ready to leave your body, looking down on your half collapsed shell, gradually dying.

Hearing Hestia's tales, Irisa had been grateful to live in their little village with its cliffs and sea, hill and lush valleys, and for the hours she spent learning with Fugra and Amara, she never dreamt that the same fate might befall her. Maybe this was where the gods had seen her and given her the power of the darkness, to try to protect the few she could when they were taken into the ships and hauled to foreign lands, over foreign seas. Irisa despised the idea of it all recurring, a new generation being taken to yet another land, with new customs and languages and to carefully hide her own self, deny the darker side of her nature. That was dangerous to her, the more she denied it, the more it would build up inside her, she did not want to hurt people who did not deserve it but she knew she would have to let the darkness out soon or it would overwhelm her, then she may never be herself again.

*****

They spent the night under the trees, one fire for them all, a meagre ration of some sort of hard bread, cheese, nuts and a cup of water, then they were ordered to sleep. As the morning dawned, there was much bustle between some of the slavers who had decided they would descend to shore, they appeared to be rigging ropes at stages down towards the beach, a huge man, could faintly be seen at the base of the cliffs and it was Aleixo she recognised at the top. The villagers did not share that if they walked a further mile or two there was a path that the fishermen used, yes it was still within the cliffs but they had worn the path through the caves that linked together and they had footholds used over hundreds of years by the fishermen trudging up and down the cliffs. It was the one setback of living here, but they had a whole village close by, formed near the freshwater lakes, the sea for food so they accepted it as part of their daily life and led it without murmur or complaint. However they knew that sharing their knowledge would mean they would be on the ships even sooner, so tried to avoid that possibility for as long as they possibly could. The thought of being trapped inside a wooden prison on the ocean terrified many of the villagers, only the fishermen amongst them were unconcerned about the ocean.

Pero and the others were roughly forcing

everyone to stand, pulling them out of the dust. It was still early but the sun was on the rise, within the hour the sky would be clear and bright and the heat would draw sweat from every pore of their bodies and the air would scorch their throats. The men were removed from their yokes so they could descend in a single line, they were too scared to run. Imbargalas were close and ready with muskets and knives and needed very little excuse to use them. It seemed to the Alladians that they worshipped one god but didn't think there would be any repercussions from that god when they committed sins, either the Imbargalas god was weak or it was not watching its people well.

The women were left free of yokes but herded together like cattle and forced into groups. Children screaming out as they were pushed closer ever still to the dark grey cliffs. Irisa could make out Pero moving along the line of women, sneering, picking on the young and the weak, dragging them up by limbs and hair, threatening them as he had her the day before, grabbing at their breasts, back sides, sneering sexual comments into their ears as he roped them up, getting aroused by the power it gave him, she could see his tented trousers and seethed internally.

'I will let you see the most vile of the monstrous before our time together ends, I will be the end of you Pero.'

'Hush girl,' moaned Fugra, 'Are you stupid? Don't let him hear your gift, hide it well, there will be time for him, it will come, but he doesn't need to know it!'

By the time the first slave had started to descend, they had been travelling for many days, hungry, thirsty and exhausted. The golden sand whipped up from the beach below and the dust from the cliffs above blew heavily in their faces, blinding them and making finding any footholes difficult and dangerous.

The dust and sand found its way into every pore of their skin, eyes, throats. Irisa could feel its grainy effervescence, the grains slowly moving towards her lungs, making her cough until her throat bled. There was nowhere they could stop for water, the descent had begun and they were clinging to the sharp hard rock with every fibre of their being.

The slavers had tried to peg ropes into the cliff to use as a guideline down and if she was honest this had helped but some stones were slick with blood.

They had all been barefoot for days, walking across hard ground to reach this part of the coast, their feet, already raw and blistered, had hit the rocky outcrops of rock and soaked them with hot crimson red blood.

They moved slowly, tied together in their small groups, terrified that they would all fall. Irisa positioned herself between Fugra and Amara so they could cling together. She felt Fugra struggle although the old crone would not admit it, she was terrified of the height of the cliffs.

Amara flinched as she heard a muffled scream, one of the groups had fallen, slaves, slavers, as equal as one another in death as they should have been in life. She prayed to Callias, god of the clouds to help ease their souls skywards. She was startled back to herself by a loud shout.

'Stop Pero! Stop!' screamed Aleixo, 'Let's get the rest of them back up, we're all going to die trying to get down here!'

'No, that's what these bastards want, for us to give in! The longer we're with them out here on their land, the more chance they'll have to attack us.'

'Stop this now! There is no fucking conspiracy! I command you and this group and you will do what I say, Please Pero, I want us to survive this, we have cheated death before, let's not risk getting on its wrong side.'

Irisa heard Pero sigh and his tone of voice changed.

'I will never forget that my friend, never. OK, let's get them all back up, no one left alive at the bottom,I'll cut the rope,at least then the bodies will be washed away.

The sharp black rocks cut into their feet, the searing heat cut into their raw skin, the gritty sand rasping at their eyes. They were exhausted, panting and praying silently for either an end to the descent or an end to themselves. They clung to the rocks and one another, hanging on to life by the roots, trying not to lose their footing. It was with relief that their feet found the solid ground at the top of the cliffs.It was easier for the women to grapple with the rock and cling to one another. Slaves and Imbargalas lay exhausted, sweat soaked, coughing the sand that filled their throats up and out of their lungs, glad they had survived the terrible death of being crushed on the rocks hurtling to the ground.They decided it would be a good time to stop after all the dramatic events of the climb and the loss of the slaves.

Vasconcelous was not a kind man and would want recompense for any slave that was lost. With a sense of dread of what he would have to face when he reached the ship, Aleixo set his men to sorting a rough camp,building fires, sending men to catch whatever fish they could. The slaves were given permission to move about or sit as they pleased, there were plenty of men who formed a rough perimeter, there was nowhere for them to go anyway. This didn't mean that they were totally free, the men were still in yokes, any movement was difficult, having to coordinate with another was too much for many and they sat or laid wherever they fell.

Aleixo went along the line, checking the slaves, he'd had 147 at the start of this trip, now only 139 remained, the others lost to the sea. He could hear some of the slavers moaning, he knew they were paid a pittance and knew that once they boarded the ship their resentment would grow as they would see themselves treated no better than the slaves themselves. Fights and mutinys were common he knew but resentment would be just another killer amongst the sweats, fevers and diseases or god forgive, the plague that could take away their profits.

Some of the Africans that had been taken as

slaves had been sold to them by their tribal leaders, labelled as 'those who committed sin against fellow Africans.' transportation worked well as a threat and punishment. Aleixo felt this was unfair, many he saw had not committed a crime but rather not agreed with their leaders. Pero however thought it splendid, voicing that it was no different than committing a crime in Portugal and being hanged for it.

Several of these had been good slaves and good men and they remained free from chains or yokes, being used as servants to the slavers themselves. When they reached the coast they would swell the number of sailors on board and would be treated the same as the sailors already working on the ship, resentment would mutate to anger and Aleixo knew he would have to watch Pero who would be quick to right what he saw as injustice because they were slaves and black.

Aleixo had yet to inform the men that these slaves would be squashed head to toe into the already cramped holds, meaning that there was nowhere for them to hang their small hammocks and although they had moaned continuously about their discomfort on the trip to Africa, on the return there would be even less. They faced weeks of lying on the cold, hard deck, sleeping out in all weathers, soaked, freezing or burnt depending on where they were heading.

There was no need to upset them yet, he'd wait until they actually reached the cliffs, no going back then, they'd have to sail or be left to face the wrath of the survivors of those who they had stolen, or he may let Father Francesco tell them. He'd accompanied them to turn all to god, the Barbarys had been grateful that they'd not seen much of him on the voyage out, he'd struggled with nausea and stayed in his cabin. The Barbarys saw this as a sign that his God had little faith in him, so his sermons when he did try, were brushed away or laughed off. There were a few other catholics within the crew who sought him out for sunday prayers, or when a slave or crew member died. As strong as Father Francisco thought himself, nothing had prepared him for the viscous greediness with which one part of humanity treated another and could not accept that God was the cause. He'd begun to struggle with his faith seeing the way the slaves were treated and that no God, no higher power intervened.

Irisa was wandering amongst the trees, picking at the herbs she found amongst them, seeing what would be useful to take with them on the voyage. She was plucking out radiant yellow flower buds from the honey bushes that she found.

Aleixo quietly ambled up to her. ‘What are you doing?’

She jumped, surprised by his presence, stumbled on the roots of the bush and began to fall backwards. Aleixo grabbed her hand and pulled her forward, she flew into his chest. There was a moment more than felt comfortable and she stepped back purposefully. ‘Thank you’ she muttered.

‘So apart from trying to impale yourself on this bush, what are you doing?’ he asked with a slight smile.

‘I’m collecting flower buds, this is a good herb for settling stomachs. I’m not sure how many of our people will feel ill on the ship.’

Aleixo stared into her endless dark eyes, so dark he felt he could fall into them, pools that could see all the way to another world. Aleixo looked away, when he looked back, she was smirking.

‘Well I think you had better gather as many as you can, it’s a long voyage, it’s cramped and even some of our men were ill on the way here, we’re either sailors or fishermen and used to smaller boats.

There were a fair few stomachs that did not stay full.'

He smiled at Irisa and she felt that the sun had landed on her face, the warm glow spread across her skin and into her body. How could someone so evil seem to be so full of warmth and light? Irisa did not like her thoughts to be confused. This man owned her, she was nothing to him, no more than a pig or a cow or a bottle of their porto wine anyway, so why did she feel he'd singled her out to be gentle with, to feel he was talking to her as a person, not as a slave.

'Mmm, I'll bear that in mind. Fugra, Amara and I have been gathering what we can and we are grateful we are allowed to bring our own medicines with us, they will be a help to all of us at times I'm sure.'

"We have a ships' surgeon on board, he'll deal with any major injuries. Some of the men won't trust your remedies. By morning we'll start pushing forward. I think we'll round the bay tomorrow and the cliffs will be easier to descend, then we can walk along the shoreline, it's only a few miles to where the big ships are moored.'

Fugra approached the couple tentatively, hanging back. Aleixo thought this out of politeness, Irisa knew it was so she could hear what was being said.

'Young one' Fugra pointed to Aleixo, 'Many of the people you have ripped from their homes, have no clothes, no shoes, they will get infections if they are not treated. Can I help those who need it? I will be swift.'

'Is there really a need?' he sighed, knowing what his men would say, especially Pero.

Fugra snorted, how stupid could Imbargalas be? They would let their bodies rot and fester rather than be touched 'by one of them' she would not offer again, there was a pride in being a wise woman and she had no intention of demeaning herself in front of these arse witted idiots.

Leave them then, it's your ship they'll stink out with disease! It's your ship that will have people being eaten alive by rot as the disease spreads inside their bodies all the way to their innocent souls! No skin off my nose, do as you please, you will anyway. Ghaboun alfian!'

Fugra continued to stare at Aleixo, he felt like she was challenging him, his men were stretching their necks from where they rested, trying to squint against the sun, leaning in towards the pair to pick up what was being said.

'What did you say? What do those words mean?'

Irisa faced Fugra sternly, 'Fugra please, don't give them cause to hurt any more of us, this one may not but others are baying for us to be hung, leave it be!'

Irisa turned to face Aleixo with a smile, 'Take no offence, she is tired and worried about our people.'

'Well I'll tell you exactly what she said!' shouted the usually timid Amara. 'She called you a stupid rat!' Amara spat the words out, Aleixo stood back shocked.

'I have treated you as fairly as I can old woman' he said, facing all three and shaking his head. 'If I do more, they'll lynch me, get rid of me and someone with less heart and sense will take my place and then there will be no mercy for slave, slaver or sailor, I can tell you that for certain!'

Irisa came forward, placing her hand on Aleixo's arm. 'Please,' she whispered. 'Fugra is right about infection, we know it can travel from a wound, silently through the body until it reaches the heart and stops it. Surely you need to take as many of us as you can if you want to earn your precious coins.'

Aleixo turned to face her, 'If only you knew all, if only you could see past me as the one who took you and your friends, you would see...' He stopped, he could not, should not and would not give them any explanations, they would not want to hear it, anyway it was no different to their story, but they were not stealing his people. He sighed, feeling the full weight of responsibility on his shoulders, the tone of his voice changed, stern now and sharp.

'Do as you need, crone, but you only have until my men have eaten and had small beer to finish, those who are not treated can stay as they are, or you can stop now, sit and rest like the others.'

Fugra did not answer but took her small drawstring bag and scuttled off, starting to work on the worst that were visible to her. Those who called out to her, she left, they still had breath, there was still hope for them but not those who sat and were still, sweating or gazing into the shimmering air. After their initial reluctance, those who had started to feel the effects of infection were readily letting her treat them.

Pero stormed over,'What the fuck are you letting that Crone do? She'll be poisoning them so that we don't have slaves to take back! His voice rose to a crescendo, angry with Aleixo that he could be showing these savages kindness.

'She's even got the audacity to put those dirty

stinking hands onto our men! For the love of God man, are you mad! Make her stop, Now!'

'Pero, she is just treating the most injured, unless you want them to die, if you do that's fine, I'll ask her to stop but I'll take every guinea that's lost from your share when we get back.'

'You bastard! You love them don't you! You have to be the good one even here don't you! The kind one, do you think they'd do the same for us? You know they wouldn't, you know they didn't.'

So caught up in their argument were they that they neither noticed that Fugra had crept up close to Pero and reached out to his hand. Pero jumped and shook the old woman off of him.

'Fuck off you dirty whore! You dare to touch me! I will stick this knife into your belly and rip your guts out! Fuck off and take your potions with you!'

Fugra let go of his hand but did not move. She instead pointed to his hand and shook her head.

'What is she doing?' he asked Aleixo.

'I don't know, wait what is wrong with your hand?'

Pero looked down at his right hand, the back was swollen, red and puffy, his fingers fat and pulsing against his skin. He looked sheepishly at Aleixo. 'I do not have a fever, let me be!'

Fugra again pointed to his hand, shook her head and mimed cutting her throat. Irisa stepped forward, losing patience with the angry, vile idiot that stood before Fugra, looking at her like she was a bug crawling on his skin.

Irisa managed to pick up some of the words the men spoke and in halting Portuguese explained that Fugra said that he had poison in his blood from the wound and would lose the hand or his life if she did not treat it straight away.

Pero laughed hard in their faces, 'You might have fooled this idiot,' he shouted, pointing at Aleixo,'but not me! You want me to trust you so you can give me some of that smelly shit from your bag that will kill me faster than this wound. A dip in salt water, it'll be fine.'

Fugra threw her hands up in the air and walked back to the rocks she and Amara had perched on. Irisa and Amara followed behind her. Aleixo watched them go, then turned to his friend, angry at his attitude and lack of self-care.

'You should have let her treat you, I'd have let her treat me if it meant saving my life, how'd you do it anyway?'

'I scraped it on those fucking cliffs, wasting all my energy on a half climb down and then all the fucking way up again, just because some of them fell and died! Then I got bitten by something as we rested in the grass! Why can't we just get to the ships? I am ready for home now Aleixo, I hate this fucking bug infested boiled part of the Earth, get me back to the sea!' He kicked at the dusty, stony ground with his boots, venting his anger down through his toes.

'That's the aim Pero, that's the aim, let's hope the old woman isn't right and you survive to get there my friend.'

'You are so fucking gulable! I am a fisherman, bigger fish have bitten me and I've survived, let's just get going at first light.'

The night temperatures plummeted and the slaves huddled together as best they could, the Imbargalas had a fire but they kept it's heat to themselves, nor did they share their blankets, which actually looked quite warm. The weaver women amongst them admired the cloth used, a warm type of woollen cloth that made beautifully soft blankets, so different from the coarse woven blankets they used, made from thick twine spun into cloth.

Irisa lay flat on her back, looking up to a myriad of the brightest stars as they burst through the darkness, watching them glisten and glint in and out. They reminded her of tiny fireflies in the sky. Seeing the skies calmed her, they were constant, they did not change, wherever she was she looked to the sky and the same stars shone down on her and she knew that anyone left in Allada might be looking at those stars and thinking about the ones who had been stolen, grateful to still be in the valley. Amara softly snored, her arm draped across Irisa. Fugra was sitting up, checking what was still in the medicine bag,wrapping flowers they had picked to help against sickness once on the sea.

Not one of them got much sleep or rest, too busy thinking what the next sunrise would bring, trying to work through their loss, grief and all that had happened to them. Their whole lives gone in one swoop, to be owned as a slave and what that might bring them.

As the morning broke and the light filtered down through the sky onto the cliffs and the people below, Aleixo gave a small nod of assent, Pero smiled, stomping up and down the line of slaves, shouting

'Get up! Get up! You lazy bastards, get walking!'

Aleixo watched Pero go, he hoped with all his heart his friend was wrong because despite all his bravado, Aleixo knew he had a heart in there and that he would be lost without his 'brother' whatever the others thought. He jogged along the dusty cliff edge and caught up with him, leaving slavers at the back to get the women together and moving. Perhaps Pero was right, perhaps he was too kind to these people, they would stab him in the back as soon as they were given the opportunity, he would do the same in their situation but there was no need to befriend them until they reached the ship, he was their master and they had to obey his commands, wasn't this how this slavery thing worked? He was unaware of his mind tussling with his thoughts and his conscience as he hurried the slaves along, constantly looking out to sea, his heart and mind back in Nossa Senhora de Luz.

The sun quickly moved high into the atmosphere, a huge orange orb, scorching their flesh and drying their throats as the group were forced ceaselessly onwards. With the small amount of food and water given to them, many struggled to keep moving forward. Several times they were forced to stop as a slave or slaver alike became a victim of sunstroke, dehydration or starvation.

Chapter 13- Magra.

Magra had been in pain since she had been violently assaulted back in the village. She had been too terrified to let anyone know about the intense pain in case they tried to rip the baby from her belly, so she suffered in silence. She knew that had she already been on the plantation,she would have given birth in her hut and been back out in the fields the next day, there would be no option of not getting the work done, but she was not on a plantation and in Allada the women cared for one another after childbirth and would have let her rest for the last few weeks of her pregnancy, then given her time with her safely swaddled new one before she had to get back to village chores.

Magra knew that although Fugra, Irisa and Amara would help, there would be no rest, time cost the slavers money, they wanted to force them on a monstrous ship, all the quicker to exchange them for their precious coins and to be on their way as quickly as they could. They wouldn't wait for a woman to give birth, after all, to them she was no more than a sack of spices to sell. She felt another contraction ripple through her taut body and began gritting her teeth against it. She tried to push herself off the ground, to keep moving but her body wouldn't let her. The next wave came and was stronger, it came with hot fluid leaking down her legs. She collapsed onto the gravel and dust path which was as hot and parched as she was. As the next wave ensued she cried out, then hastily placed her hand over her mouth, knowing that silence kept you safe, but it was too late, several of the group had noticed and were trying to get her help. She laid on the floor, giving into the pain and sensation that was tearing her body apart, she couldn't move, let them kill her but she couldn't move.

Magra cradled her stomach, the prominent bulge of her unborn infant. An Imbargala was coming closer to her, she flinched, what would he do in punishment? What would happen to her? With one hand on her belly and one hand held up to gesture stop, she gave in, supplicating and pleading, gesturing to the Imbargala not to hurt her. She faded away,gripped in pain, only faintly aware that the Imbargala was Aleixo, would he be kind now? The long awaited pause for the violence to start didn't yield anything. Aleixo stood over her awkwardly, trying to gesture with his hands, asking if the baby was coming. She nodded at him and sighed, at this point although he had stolen her from her village, allowed his men to assault her and made her treck miles in the overbearing heat of the day, she felt blessed that he had not hurt her and it seemed he had no intention of doing so.

He took off his linen jacket and wrapped it into a ball, placing it under her head as a pillow and gestured he would get help. With a swift purposeful gait he made his way to the crone and her friends. He hadn't even reached them before he began shouting out to them.

'I need you three now!'

Fugra spat on the scorched earth, 'Now he needs us! Well he can fuck off!'

He stood breathless in front of them, miming a heavily pregnant belly and shaking his head and holding his hands in the air. Irisa gazed at Amara and Fugra, imploring them with her eyes and with concern.

'Magra? Oh no it's Magra, it's all my fault Fugra, this is because of me!' tears soaked her face, dripped down and sizzled into the hot ground.

'Irisa keep yourself together, we need to see her and see if the baby is in danger, quick now girl!'

Amara and Irisa ran back to the huddled mass on the floor, with Fugra tottering behind with the leather medicine sack. Irisa was full of trepidation as she homed in on Magra who was writhing on the hard dusty floor, obviously bleeding, she knelt by her side, trying to calm her.

Aleixo leant over her, ‘Can you help? Will she live?’

‘Live! You pigs did this! The bastard that kicked her in the stomach did this! We will be lucky to have one alive after this. Let alone both. I suppose you are worried you’ll lose your precious coins for her body!’

Aleixo sighed, he could perfectly understand why this old witch felt the way she did, he would have spoken to the Moors the same way if he had had the chance, but he truly did care if this woman lived or died or delivered a live child. They did not know it but he had a heart, yes explaining to Vasconcelos that they had lost two slaves due to him not controlling his men would sting but he did not want to be responsible for the loss of any other lives, he realised now how naive he had been to accept the commission but there was nothing he could do now accept to beg these women to do what they could.

Irisa touched his hand, ‘We will do all we can,

please get us as much cloth as you can, clean if possible, if not anything and water, or wine, Magra needs something.'

Aleixo ran, shouting at the men to hand over their shirts, he swept back to them with a bundle of rough cloth, linen and blankets, wine and water skins. Fugra took charge as they sat themselves around the woman who was crying and clinging to her stomach, attempting to keep the baby safe within.

'Help me Fugra! I can't have this baby now, they will take it away and kill it, Please!' she let out an intense cry of pain, 'the baby is coming but something is wrong, I can't push.' She screamed again as a contraction tore through her body.

'Magra, calm, it is too late for that now, this baby is on the way, you will bear this, we need to do what we can to make sure you are here to care for the small one, think no further than that.'

Irisa and Amara sifted through the cloth, finding the cleanest pieces which they ripped into strips, opening out another as a sheet to swaddle the baby.

'Amara, go into the medicine bag, there is Intsenga in there, give Magra some leaves to chew on to relax her, give her water. I will examine her with Irisa.' Amara acknowledged her with a slight nod of the head and retrieved the leather bag, heavy with medicine, pulling the long silky leaves out of the bag and passing them to Magra.

'Come Magra, try and chew this, it will help you.'

Magra put the leaves to her lips and pushed them into her mouth, as she began to chew and feel the sickly sap from the leaves lining her throat she began to relax, to feel a sense of calm that she had not felt before, a disconnection from her body that aided her tolerating her bodies attack.

'Irisa, promise me you will save the baby, I don't want to be here if the baby is taken away from me, I couldn't bear it.'

Irisa soothed her sweaty brow and bade her drink from the water skin. 'You will be here yourself my friend but I promise you I will do all I can to protect this child if you no longer can.'

Fugra lifted Magras tunic, it was obvious she was haemorrhaging, this was not the usual blood of imminent birth. She wiped her hands across her face and turned away to whisper to Irisa and Amara, ' She is in danger and so is the child, we must cut her. Give her wine Irisa, then ask the Imbargalas for a sharp knife, we will cleanse it with fire.'

Irisa walked to where the men had gathered and approached Aleixo. Without hesitation he gave her his own knife and walked to the fire the men sat around. She propelled the knife into the white hot flames and after a minute or two returned to Fugra.

'Irisa, she has had Intsenga, give her more wine and hold her down, this is going to hurt her. Amara, gather twine and a needle, I will need to sew her and we will need to bind her. The men all turned away, distancing themselves from the death they might have incurred, for all their bravado, seeing it this close was unsettling, some were scared of the blacks and the witch women and were waiting for some curse or another to befall them, believing as each scream left Magras labouring mouth, she was cursing them and their families. As Fugra put the knife to Magra she prayed to her ancestors, to Mami Water - mother and healer, to Takhar, god of justice to avenge whatever might befall this mother and child.

Magra gave a harsh, loud scream as the hot knife slid along her flesh before falling silent as she passed out with pain. Fugra cut deep and swift, throwing the knife down as she slid her hands into the open maw of Magras flesh. She fumbled until she felt the firm flesh of the baby and pulled, shouting ;swaddling'

Amara spread the cloth on the floor, Fugra passed the blood covered tiny bundle to Amara who wrapped it first in linen and then in a warm blanket, no sounds came from the cherub, silent, tiny bluish lips pursed together. Amara quickly turned the bundle over,hitting his back until he emptied the fluids from his lungs onto the ground and squalled loudly. Amara walked off to the shade of the trees with the water skin to clean the tiny male child.

Fugra rubbed her hands on the strips by her hands and picked up the needle and thick twine and began to pull Magras flesh back together with crude stitches. She swathed the wound in a foul smelling paste made from devil's claw and centrella, she soaked the remaining cloth in water and cleaned Magra as best as she could, covered her with a blanket to rest, then finally sat back sighing.

Only when Magra was covered did Aleixo return to the group, 'How goes it crone?'

'The child lives, at the moment Magra needs sleep and rest, she will not be able to walk, you either carry her or kill her but I can do no more.'

‘Will she recover?’

"Given time and medicine, yes, but not by this evening or tomorrow, if you give her a chance to live, you will have two slaves to sell at the end of your travels Imbargala.’

Aleixo scratched his chin, wiped the sweat from his brow. What would be the best outcome for him? For Vasconcelos? He faced Fugra, ‘Do what you can, we will rest here now until morning, can we move her then? I fear I can’t make the men wait any longer than that.’

‘Yes, with help I will try, we will need more water, wine and blankets.’

‘You will have what you need, don't worry, witch woman.’

Amara cooed over the baby who was calm and quiet, warm and healthy, thankfully Magra had been close to delivery or the outcome could have been very different after the slaver maliciously kicked her stomach and ruptured her, luckily neither had died, although the next twenty four hours would be critical for them both. Amara went off to the group of women and children, finding another mother Maria- who had recently birthed a child, and asked her if she would feed the baby, which she did gladly and offered to be on hand until Magra came too and could feed the little one herself.

Irisa, Amara and Fugra gathered by the sleeping Magra, she slept lightly but at least her body was resting. The women laid down beside Magra, slowly their eyes began to close and they drifted away to the land of dreams where they could be free, mind,body and soul.

Chapter 14-Women's Work.

Irisa came back from the world of sleep reluctantly, she had been bone tired and although cold, uncomfortable and hungry, at least she had been resting. The smell of the damp, dewy earth found its way into her nose, she inhaled the scent deeply, sensing it fill her with comfort and ease, knowing that this may well be the last day she ever smelt Allada again. The weak morning light had started to wake the Imbargalas who had begun to pack their kit, ready for the last part of the earthbound journey, ready to transition to the sand and the vast ocean in front of them. As a gentle breeze moved through the group, Irisa could sense the salt in the air and began to anticipate what the next part of their journey would bring. She stood and stretched. Magra was sleeping peacefully and had since the birth of the baby, whom she was then on her way to fetch from the village woman who had fed him through the night. She trudged through the dust to find Maria.

She was sitting with her back to a rock, the newborn swaddled tight in the old linen shirt, he was held to her breast, his soft curls brushing her skin, he was suckling well.

Irisa sat down heavily, Maria looked up and smiled, 'How is Magra?'

'Well she made it through the night, she is sleeping but just starting to wake, I thought i'd bring the babe to her as she woke up. Has he fed well so far?'

'He is a little greedy' she said giggling, 'He is a dear little cherub, so small yet he had a mighty voice and a mighty thirst and that bodes well for his future.' As he lulled in his suckling, Maria moved him off her breast, tightening the swaddling cloth and passed him to Irisa. 'Take him to his mother but if she is still weak I am happy to feed him' She turned away and started to fuss with her own tiny bundle.

Irisa walked slowly back, cradling him in her arms as she marvelled at his tiny puckered mouth that was trying to suckle the air,mesmerised by his tiny fingers and the deep creases in his hands that had managed to escape the swaddling. She touched his finger and he gripped tightly.

Irisa felt confused by her emotions and feelings that this tiny bundle, this tiny human seemed to have brought out of her. Her heart was his from that first moment, she knew then that she would do anything to save this little life that had helped to bring into this world. She was overwhelmed with anxiety for him. What would become of a newborn child in the arms of men such as this? Would they have him brought up as 'a thing' property to fight coin over? Would they let him live? Sea journeys were notoriously hard with young children. If he could survive would they want to profit from his sale or drop him in the ocean, one less mouth to feed? She turned all this over in her head and heart as she travelled back towards Magra, just as the rest of the group awoke and started moving about for the day ahead.

She felt an arm on hers 'Are you ok? Shall I take the babe?'

Irisa came back to herself, Amara was watching her closely, 'I think you will be a wonderful mother someday.' Irisa smiled back at her.

'I only wish I knew what our futures held Amara, what we definitely don't know is how the next part of our lives is set. We may never have the chance to have children. Let's focus on helping Magra to continue being a mother whilst we can.'

Magra had started to stir, Fugra was removing more Intsenga from the leather bag in preparation for the tea that would help with the pain of birthing the babe. Magra reached out her arms for her newborn son, ' Ahh little one, come to your Mammy, we did it, we are saved.'

'Before you get too excited madam, you need to take the tea and settle, this is going to be uncomfortable for you my dear one.'

'Do you think you could feed this little man? It will be good for him to be close to his Mammy.' Magra gave a shy smile, 'I would love to try.' she put his tiny face to her breast and he began suckling, the snuffling, snorting noises made the women smile, this baby was a fighter, he would need to be. Magra stroked the tight black curls atop his soft brown skin and kissed him. 'I will call him Teagu, after his father. He will never know his voice or his touch but he will have his name and his spirit.'

Tears glistened in the corner of her eyes. Teagu had been killed back in Allada, fighting to keep his pregnant wife from being captured. Magra felt the empty space beside her as a deep ache in her belly and heart. He had been a kind and loving man and she would now never have that again. She felt his presence most often at night and sometimes as the moon shed its soft silver sheen over the landscape, she could see his outline, him waving to her from a field of beans, happy and content.

One day she would join him and if it hadn't been for the birth of their son so early, she may already be in that field with him, but for the sake of the baby she would fight to stay with him, to protect him as best she could from the evil of slavery, slavery and torment.

'That is a strong name, I feel the father is present and will protect his namesake from the evil he could not fight in this world.' Fugra laid hands on Teagu and prayed to the gods for his protection.

Amara and Irisa had gone into the small clearing, looking for wood they could use to fashion some sort of carrier for Magra. She would not be able to walk for a day or two and they knew that the slavers would not help. They gathered the strongest of the Jambackto trunks and made their way back to the group. They used the blanket Magra had been given and stretched it across the wooden branches, tying it in place with twine. Fugra gathered all the medicines with her and, satisfied that Magra had finished her Intsenga tea and was starting to doze off, encouraged her onto the blanket.

Aleixo made his way over to Irisa and the group

of women.'She made it through the night then? I had not dared believe it could be so.'

'Fugra has good medicines and Magra is strong, we do not give up so easily in our village.'

Aleixo blushed.' I meant no disrespect, I am just surprised, in our own town even with midwives, many women died in childbirth, I am simply surprised at her survival.'

"We have a long way to go yet, we have made a carrier for Magra, she can not walk today, we will manage it between us, it is no bother to us.'

Aleixo smiled 'how industrious you are, I have never seen women working together like this, it warms the heart,'

'It is the only way we can survive here, we need each other to get through the harsh days and nights our country sends us . We do not have others who care for us like your soft women, we take pride in being strong and not giving in.'

'Maybe you can teach some of my men then, or the mariners when we get to the ships, many are bone idle, whilst others work until their fingers are red and sore to the bone.'

'Mmm because you work for yourselves, to get what you want just for you. When you share the load, it becomes lighter.'

Aleixo nodded, his soft caramel curls bouncing around his face, Irisa could not help but look as the brightening sun glistened across his vivid eyes. 'We need to get moving, I'll get everyone together.'

As he walked away, she watched him go, willing him to turn and notice her, longing for him to single her out for attention. Then she scolded herself, what was she thinking? Why would he? A Portugese Imbargala, here to take her liberty, her friends, her life if need be, why would he turn to see her? But he did, just as he reached the men, he turned and smiled.

The slaves were marched through the increasingly dusty, sandy path, the cerulean sea glistening, now visible on their right. How they wished themselves in that sea as the cool waves lapped against their sore and dusty skin, washing away the pain of leaving others behind, washing away the fear or the new world they did not wish to be a part of but they had no choice other than to face.

As they rounded the cliff, they came across a bay with a sharp incline down onto the white sandy shore. Crabs scuttled in groups, flurrying sideways about their business with complete ignorance to the pheromones emitting from the terrified slaves.

Their bright shells glinted in the sunlight, slick with water they looked almost golden. The waves lapped viciously against the white sand, churning it up, spraying foam and seaweed as it retreated back into the sea.

Irisa inhaled deeply, she felt her soul lift, it belonged to the sea, to the shore, and to the creatures that lurked beneath the rocks, the bright green waves topped with white fluffy foam, how would she survive away from it?

They soon began to spy what looked like large wooden buildings on the shore and two ships anchored a little way out from the beach. Her heart sank. So, they were at their next prison, soon even the sun and the daylight would be stripped from their possession, they would be entitled to nothing, she felt a shiver through her body as her imagination ran wild with how it would be aboard this floating prison. What had caught the eye of the other slaves wasn't the sea or the ships but the forts that had been built on the foreshore. They could faintly see Imbargalas guarding the perimeter and had begun to gabble between themselves, the mood of the group moving from solemn to fractious.

Two of the men yoked together tried to run, they knew the fate that awaited them in those forts, those slave factories and they had no intention of making it through those gates, so they did, shouting to one another, 'Faster, Vinnigir!'

Irisa and Amara looked across to one another in fear, hearing the Portuguese shouting 'stop!' but they didn't stop, they kept running, the sweat pouring from their bodies, glistening dark brown, clammy from the heat, the whites of their eyes large, open like frightened dogs. The Imargalas were closing in, there was no escape.

The women heard ' Stop now or we will shoot!'

'Vinnigir! Vinnigir!'

But one of the men slipped on the dusty ground and they both fell hard onto a rocky outcrop, then two loud shots rang out, the noise deafening the slaves, many who had not heard a weapon fired before, thinking it thunder that had struck the men, Both fell down, blood oozing from the holes in their heads, their eyes now glazed and unmoving.

'Anyone else?'

There was a silence so heavy, so dense it was hard to break, the slaves huddled together on the floor, the women covering one anothers heads as if they could stop the momentum of a metal bullet with their will alone. Pero stood straddling the two dead men, men who had simply not wanted to be slaves, not wanting to get on a ship to a world they didn't know and wouldn't understand, men who wanted to live as free men.

'I said, anyone else? You are now the property of Vasconcelos, you have no rights other than those he chooses to give you. If you do as we say, you will live, it is that simple, but we will get you into those slave forts and we will be taking you to the ships, is that clear?'

Many of the slaves nodded their heads in agreement, while others looked down, they could not face the stony eyes of those pig slavers, they knew they could not fight them, so they kept their pride and kept their eyes and heads down. Pero started using his rifle to prod at people, forcing them up onto their feet.

'Look down to the shore, that's your home for the next couple of days. We are going now and you will have to obey me, do you hear?'

Weary, dust covered, skin abraded by the sand blowing from the bay, the exhausted slaves set off for the final part of their land journey. The men, women and children were separated, each making their way towards one of the forts, pressed together like fish in a shoal, the scent of sweat, urine, shit and vomit so strong it was difficult to inhale any air.

Chapter 15- The Cleansing

Amara, Irisa and Fugra stayed as close together as they could, apart from Magra who had been taken with the others who'd recently given birth or were pregnant. They were jostled into the wooden prison. Alexio had managed to slip away from the crew unnoticed and assured the women they would not be here long before they were taken onto the ships where there would be a little more light and air. As they were forced into the fort, they were arranged in single file, each one made to remove their clothes, a disinterested young man and what seemed to be an ancient old woman let their presence be known coldly, examining each one in turn.

They were afforded no privacy, stood naked in their flesh, prodded as livestock would be. The old woman babbled to the boy who wrote down each of their names, their age and condition. They may as well have been a cargo of sugar, evaluated and sold. Amara was distraught at taking off her clothes in front of all these people, she was sweating as she tried to cover her breasts with her hands.

'I wouldn't worry about covering those,' laughed the Crone, 'wait till I examine your cunt!'

The boy sneered and eyed Amara lasciviously.

'Name' she shouted.

'My name is Amara, from Allada.'

'Well isn't that wonderful, you won't be seeing that again! Now you seem ripe for marriage, have you been cut yet?'

'No, there was no need, I have not had a match in my village, so my mother said I didn't have to.'

'Well, you have no fucking choice here, Vasconcelous wants maximum gold for those of you he can, so you will do what is right and be cut! I'm not giving him dirty whores whom he can't sell when he gets here. Give me any cause for concern that you think fucking another slave is a good idea and i'll not just cut you, i'll sew you up so tight you won't be able to piss straight,'

Amara started to cry gently, the thought of a stranger touching her was improper, unthinkable, how could it make her worth more?

Irisa moved forward in the cue and reached out to her friend, the boy kept in front of her.

'Get your filthy hands of her you slut! The only people who touch her now are those she's sold to, so get back in line or I'll shoot you, you filthy shit'

Irisa moved back, she felt bile rise in her throat,

felt acid burning her gullet. She swallowed it back, feeling her heart beating faster, sensing the darkness consuming her heart, trying to take over her body, to leap and reap the revenge they could feel she craved. She calmed herself, knowing there would be a time that was right, when she could wield her dark power over these savages, she would make sure she felt all the disgust, hate and violence that herself and the villagers had been subjected to and she would unleash hell on the earth they stood upon. For now, she knew she had to take what they did and accept it without letting them know the anger in her heart.

'Jose, put this one down for cutting, take her to the side, these filthy peasants are not worthy of Vasconcelous's customers like this, he'll take it out on me and you, he can be a cruel bastard when he's not got his own way.'

Jose grunted, made a mark against Amaras name and shoved her to one side.

Irisa moved forward in the cue, undressed without complaint and allowed the old crone to shove her fingers sharply inside her, she felt around her, smiling as she did so. Irisa made sure no expression showed on her face, looking straight at the crone with clear eyes.

'Like it do you?' She gave a throaty laugh. 'Another one Jose! Their village must have been filled with unnatural acts, we'll have to watch them on the ship. This one needs cutting too.'

And so it went on as dozens of women were subjected to harrowing assaults hidden as medical examinations to make sure they were fit and healthy for the trip. They stood for hours. Shoved together, no water, the heat building in the poorly ventilated wooden forts they were shoved into. There were no buckets, they had no choice but to piss and shit on the floor where they stood.

Finally the little light that had filtered through the building turned a dusty pink and the last of the women were brought in. There was now a group of about thirty who held one another, hiding their shame and embarrassment, they saw a huddled figure pushing through the crowd, it was not until they heard a rough voice cursing that they realised it was Fugra. Tears streamed down their faces as they held one another. Fugra stood herself up,

'Come on, enough of that, that won't get us anywhere, now calm yourselves, if we are going to survive this we will stay strong, we can do this.'

Irisa looked closely at Fugra, 'Forgive me for

saying this but how did you come to be in with the young uncut women? Forgive me but you are old, you must have been cut years ago!'

Fugra gave the deepest laugh they had heard from her, ' Oh my! I gave you two more credit, of course it's been years since my cutting you fools.I managed to convince that old woman that I could help with the healing of the cuttings, she was some sort of wisewoman in her village before she was stolen herself and made to work for this evil shit, so she knew it made sense, I convinced her if she wanted us to be worth as much as possible, she needed to use me well.'

'Oh Fugra, I thank all the Gods for you being with us, I don't think we could bear it without you.'

They were left cold,hungry, smelling and scared. The night became the black of charred wood, no light, no heat and as the temperature plummeted they began shivering, huddling together for warmth. There was noise though, a gentle keening filled the room, people softly sobbing or praying. The sound was rhythmic, soothing to Irisa who despite the trauma, drifted off to sleep.

The morning began early. The soft dawn light had yet to breach the horizon. They were made to stand, each was given a simple tunic to put over their cold, dirty bodies. The women were shoved into groups, the older ones were marched out of the fort, to where they did not know and they were not told.

The Crone from the day before appeared and stood before the group of the uncut that were left.

'So this fine morning, you become respectable according to tradition. My name is Areila and I will be cutting. Do as I say and you will be fed and moved to the ship, disobey, try to run, the men outside will kill you. Maybe they'll rape you first but they will kill you. That makes Vasconcelous mad, one less coin to earn, be sensible, survive.'

She made her way towards the back of the large space they were in. They had not noticed in the dark that there was a pallet bed on the floor and a small wooden table covered with instruments, rusty and old, alongside a bowl of water and a bundle of rags, she came forward and grabbed Fugra roughly.

'This witch, you all know, she will be helping so your cunts don't end up a pussy mess. Let's hope you trust her, poison in the blood is not a good way to die, trust me, I see it often enough.'

She turned and moved to the bed and until it was her turn they did not see her again.

A stream of young women could be heard screaming, despite the stick they had been given to bite down on. Fugra had managed to make a tea from Intsentsa to help the women after with the pain and had centrella paste to put across their wounds. Irisa moved reluctantly forwards, her heart thumping. She knew this was wrong, this was not the way it should happen, she had hoped that their village would stop the cutting of its young women. Fugra had tried for many years to show it did not make them pure. Her heart sank as she realised this was the ultimate power the slavers had over the women, this meant they controlled whom she lay with, but it was more than that, if done wrong, it could cause infection sepsis and a bad death, if you survived with an altered shape, then no one would accept you as pure either, if you were stitched and those stitches ripped, which they could, you were called a whore, damned for having sex with another out of union. A woman could not win.

Would there ever be a time when women could decide what they wanted for themselves? If they wanted their labia cut from them, Irisa could not believe it.

Fugra gestured for her to lie on the bed. She

passed her a piece of branch to bite on. 'This will hurt little one forgive me for not being able to protect you.'

'Get out of the way you stupid bitch, better to just let her get on with it, much good your talk of protection will do her. Now bite girl, bite hard.'

Irisa's pupils dilated as Areila began to cut her vaginal lips with the rusty blade, she tried to take her mind elsewhere but she could smell the coppery tang of fresh blood, she could feel it oozing from her severed lips. She felt another rip as the final part was removed and she faded into blackness as unconsciousness finally held her in its arms.

She woke up to Fugra trying to pour insensate down her throat, 'Come Irisa, I have put centrella paste on the wound and used cloth to bind you. I will look after you and Amara, we are going to be taken to the ships soon, have strength.'

Irisa's eyes leaked salty tears down onto the rough tunic she now wore.

'Why do they do this? Why take us, humiliate us, deface us? Why do our gods not protect us, Fugra?'

'My little one, I know not but I believe they will, that we have to swallow our adversity, take it in hand, they will come and punish those vile pigs, trust me, Irisa my love.'

Irisa nodded, she so wanted to believe Fugra but at that point she had given up all hope and faith and wanted to pass to the other realm to be with her mother and friends back in Allada with all being well.

The golden sunlight dazzled their eyes as they left the fort, a more motley group you never did see. Some of the girls were crying and holding themselves, clearly bleeding through their bindings, others bent double with pain, still though one or two forced themselves upright and faced the slavers, forcing them towards the wooden village on the ocean.

Chapter 16- Floating Hell

The water was cold, drenching their rough tunics that were now clinging to their tender skin. The harsh sun beating down relentlessly upon their backs, stinging like whips as they moved through the azure sea, sloshing against their thighs. Struggling to stay upright, fighting against the current that seemed to be encouraging them back to shore, one last chance to reach their homeland.

The ship loomed immense and intimidating above them, never in their lives had they seen anything like this, a wooden village moving on the water. To them it was unfamiliar and terrifying. Roughly made rope ladders were thrown overboard by the mariners who'd stayed on the ship, the stench of their bodies wafting on the breeze that swept along the shore. Irisa was first to attempt the ladder, her clothes soaked, heavy with cold sea water, her body sore and bleeding, she heaved herself up each rung, her arms straining in their sockets. She was hauled on board by a heavily built mariner, his thick forearms pilling her up.

'Welcome to the Juniper my lady' he cackled. Spitting phlegm onto the deck.

‘You’re now the property of Vasconcelos, stand over there.’

Soaked and weary she trudged to where indicated, confused by the sight of another sailor who had what appeared to be a bowl of fire and a metal stick, she could smell burnt flesh and her heart filled with terror.

‘Keep still, it’ll be quick, ' he scoffed.

She had no idea what he meant but seconds later she discovered as he plunged the stick into the fire and pressed it against her arm. Her body jolted as it tensed with pain and heat and despite her resolve, she screamed as the brand melted into her skin. She was pushed to the group who waited, holding their arms, trying to stem tears, indignant, proud but confused and hurt. She looked to her fellow slaves who had been marked in the same way.

‘Why have they done this?’

‘To show we belong to Vasconcelos, look at your mark girl.’

As she did in her last moments of lucidity, she glanced at her singed, burned flesh and could make out a rough V shape on her arm. She had been branded with his mark. Irisa now no longer existed as herself , she was part of a cargo, a product without light or life.

Vasconcelos watched from the poop deck, eyeing his property as they were manhandled down into the hold. Their provisions for the middle passage would have to be shared carefully, he had removed much to fit in as many slaves as he could. He was accompanied by the ship's surgeon- William Thorpe-Evans, Vasconcelos knew him well from his gambling days in London. Evans had only been too keen to accept an offer to join the voyage on the Juniper, mounting debts and many creditors now threatening payment on pain of death, along with a scorned, vengeful wife meant he was more than happy to leave the shores of England, with hopes that by the time he returned, he'd either made his fortune or better still he would simply never see those shores again.

He charged onto deck as soon as he knew the slaves had started to board. Until then he had hid beneath the decks, within his cabin with a bucket and an infusion of ginger. He has suffered nausea the entire journey and even at anchor the rhythmic rocking of the ship made him feel slightly sick. He'd been the butt of many a joke on the outward trip and he sorely hoped he'd manage better on the return, if only to keep his pride, which he was mightily attached to.

He eyed the savages as they boarded. The men had been stored in the cargo hold, side by side, head to toe, barely room to move their bodies. He'd prayed he'd not have to go down into that dank, dark hold. He knew the stench would be unpalatable to him.

However the women were now wading through the water, making their way to the ship. He watched as their skirts rode higher in the sea, showing thighs and legs with either muscle or snew, he hoped he'd see more but the opportunity had not yet arisen. He wiped the sweat from his eyes, this godforsaken country was hotter than hell, he prayed they'd soon be feeling the sea winds whisking through the decks. He eyed the women greedily, lasciviously. He knew what he wanted. He had been promised as ship's surgeon that he was entitled to a slave, one he could own, sell or make a profit from or fuck as he wished to. Vasconcelos made it quite clear that there was nothing that one could do to a slave that was considered abhorrent. He had spent much of the journey imagining those glorious sinful acts, rubbing his cock through his britches in his cabin to pass the time.

A group of three women struggled to the deck of the ship, he watched closely as they were branded. He was intrigued by the group. One old crone was clutching a small bag, with her were two of the most beautiful negresses he'd seen. One had the most startling deep pooled eyes the colour of molasses and the other although not as classically beautiful, held herself like a princess. He thought she had a fight within her and that would make for fun and spoil his cabin.

'I claim her!' he shouted eagerly

Vasconcelos let out a hearty laugh, 'hold ye on sir! They have only just started boarding, there's many fine fillies yet.'

'You said I had a choice Captain, well I have chosen her!' He stood like a petulant child expecting to get his own way.

Vasconcelos was irritated, he'd brought this man along on the adventure, yes, but he had no liking for the man, he could be petty and mature at times.

'Do not dare to believe that as a simple acquaintance you can command me at will sir! You are simply the ship's surgeon, the barber who guts, cuts and sews! So I would hold my tongue and stem your pride if you know what's good for you!'

Evans became incensed, raising his voice to a squeal.

'Do you mean to renege on your promises Captain? I believed you to be a man of your word.'

'I am a man of my word!' yelled Vasconcelos. 'A slave you were promised and a slave you shall have but that one is not for you, she is already taken, she has been promised to our First mate, who has more about him in his little finger than you have in your simple brain god damn you!'

Unknowingly, Evans had been pointing towards Irisa, whilst unknown to her, Aleixo had already requested her to be named as his in a bid to keep safe the one person he had felt a connection with since boarding the Juniper.

'What about the one with her, she's comely, I bet she jiggles well in the sack!' he guffawed loudly.

'Well, she's young and bearable to look at for a negress, I suppose I'll claim her. Can someone bring her to me when she's cleaned up though, she looks like a bloody savage dressed like that.'

Vasconcelos looked Evans square in the eyes 'Why you imbecile, that's cos she is a fucking savage! You are a dullard at times!'

Evans looked down to the deck, why he had befriended this man at the gaming tables he had no idea, all he did was mock him and lower his status. Well he thought, let's see how he thinks of me when he needs me to sew up mangled limbs.' With a huff he'd skulked back to his cabin, highly put out that a man as low as first mate got the pick of the spoils whilst he had to have seconds. Well he'd still have her, she was a slave and whoever she belonged to, he was going to bed her when he liked and how he liked.

Chapter 17 -Stench

The women were shoved into a small space beside the stinking animal pens. The goats, pigs and chickens similarly crushed together, sounds of terror and fear emptying from their beaks, snouts and mouths. They had such little room but did not waste their time bemoaning their fate for they had heard about the conditions the men were being kept in. Many had partners who had been yoked and tied to another, shoved below deck in the dark, now probably lying in their own urine and faeces. Gods forbid what would happen when the ship started to move, none had been on anything larger than a small wooden boat, sized for a lonely fisherman and his catch, this was a world on water, one they could not begin to fathom and one they knew they would never see the whole of. A soft keening began from those grieving for ones either left behind or down below, fighting to breathe in the stale air.

The gentle sway beneath their feet caused many to struggle to walk to where they were being pushed, flailing, slipping or tumbling upon one another like rats trying to flee a flood and reach the dry shore. They were at least free, that is not shackled, they would be on deck every day once the ship was at sail, at present that seemed a blessing, they would soon find that once they were in open water that was not always the case, the weather could be a tormenting devil but at least they would have eyes upon the swirling ocean and be able to breath purer air, even if it was for a limited time.

Fugra bade Amara and Irisa to sit close to her, they pulled their legs into them, pulling their tunics around them as best they could.

'Has anyone seen Magra yet?' The women began to scan the crowded deck but could not see the new mother in their midst.

'Maybe she was chosen by the men? I heard Aleixo talking about it on the trek here. Some of the men can choose a slave, maybe that's where she is.'

The hope in Amara's voice made Fugra's heartache, 'Let us believe it girl, let us believe it.' she turned away, hoping that for now at least Amara would not see the truth in her eyes.'

The last of the women were shoved together in their small hold, akin to another animal enclosure, Irisa caught the attention of the mariners.

'Have you seen the woman on the bed we carried here? She has a newborn with her, she may need the medicines we carry with us.'

'I wouldn't be looking for her and her baby if I were you. What were we going to do with them? A half dead woman and a baby with no one to feed it! You women are a bloody nuisance and a curse to our damn boat! If you weren't worth a groat or two, I swear we'd only capture your men! We left her on the shore, she's too damaged for Vasconcelos, she's with her screaming brat, so shut up and think yourself lucky we didn't do the same to you! Accursed fucking women on a ship, madness!'

Irisa never heard the rest of his tirade, she was trying to stop her heart from pounding, breaking into pieces for they had surely left Magra and the infant to their deaths with no one to care for them. Magra would be too weak to care for the infant, within days they would be the meal of hungry animals unless those left found her. Irisa held onto Fugra and Amara's hands and they said a prayer for their friend's soul and for that of Teagu, her newborn.

They could feel the pull of the water as the ship began to move, they could hear the chatter and cursing of the mariners and the Imbargalas, celebrating their capture, until they reached the shores of the distant lands they were headed to, their work was done and for now they would assist the mariners in keeping the ship upright on the water.

Fugra spat into the air 'Filthy bastard men! They celebrate taking our homes, lives, our bodies! May they choke on their stinking beer!

There was much nodding amongst the women, those who weren't vomiting onto the wooden decks, the motion of the ship too much for them to bear. Fugra began handing out some of the herbs she had gathered, giving leaves to the women with instructions to chew. As she passed a leaf to one of the young women, she froze sensing movement from the corner closest to her. Fugra tensed and slowly turned her body expecting an attack, then realised it was Aleixo, who had fetched buckets of water and ladles for them to drink from.

'Thank you kind one, I said you would not be one of them did I not?'

He smiled at her, ' What are you doing with those leaves?'

'These help the sickness that your boat causes, we have to try something or we'll be knee deep in vomit by the end of the night.'

He laughed gently, 'I know how poor the

conditions are, I'll bring food and water when I can, I have come to speak to Irisa.'

Irisa turned her face to his and the light in her eyes felt brighter than any sun that shone on the top of the horizon.

'I have chosen you as mine, I hope this is agreeable with you?'

'Well I don't have any choice do I? You now own me, I am a belonging now, like a favourite cloth or pot! You will take me whatever I say and you will use me how you like. I have heard what some of these sea born men do to their own women, we will be treated no better than the swine we live beside.'

'I would never treat you in such a manner. I know I have little influence over Vasconcelos and the men, other than trying to remind him of the worth of your people and that it's in his best interests to feed and care for you all so he can make more money when he gets off this ship. If you are with me, no other man may touch you, you will sleep safely in my cabin. If you find the idea intolerable, I will say I made a mistake and choose another.'

He turned his head, hiding his wounded pride, he had not expected gratitude for slavery but she must understand this was all he could do to try and save her life, just one life to try and assuage his conscience.

Irisa sighed, ‘ I accept, I thank you for looking out for me, I just have a heavy heart at the thought of my friends and their fates.’

‘I’ll speak to the surgeon, he is choosing Amara, but I believe that when I explain how useful Fugra has been he will take her as well to help with the many sicknesses we’ll encounter on the voyage, he’ll be glad of the help. He has been on other voyages and is well used to medicine women, he accepts their power with herbs and healing and I believe he will be kind to her.’

Irisa nodded, ‘What happens now?’

"We get this damn lump of wood moving out onto the open sea, I will come and find you after exercise today.’

She slumped down on the floor emotionally drained. Was this her worth now? She’d been given to a man as a toy, a plaything to stop them grumbling on the journey. The sway of the ship to her was a lullaby and against all odds, laying with her back against the rough timber, she fell into a deep slumber.

She slid beneath the depth of sleep, down into

Durno's realms, the darkness enveloping her. She felt at ease down here amongst the un-avenged, the dead and yes, the evil. She felt them clawing their way through her consciousness. She breathed deeply and calmed, 'Soon, soon you'll be free and praise the gods these bastards will suffer.' She raised herself back to sleep and dreamt of nothing else but darkness.

Chapter 18- Endurance.

A daily routine soon set in on board ship and although tedious, unpleasant and more akin to surviving than living, they were at least surviving and that was a high hope indeed. Twice a day the women were brought up to exercise and move around the deck. Irisa felt grateful for these small moments, grateful to be in the fresh salty air that fizzed on her tongue, grateful to not be sitting amongst the detritus of humans and their leaves, grateful to be away from the sick and the dying.

Disease had set in early, some from wounds, some from the women who had been cut and had not healed, dying in agony from poison of the blood. Irisa helped Fugra attend to many, many people. Along with the disease came distrust, quickly rumours began to circulate that the women were witches, they had to be, the sailors saw them applying herbs, pastes, teas to the sick and the people began to heal. The Alladians did nothing to alter their perception, it meant they at least held some power over their capturs. Rather than look to the obvious , the mariners saw it as dark magic, one that came from their homeland. Many of the mariners began to accuse the wise women of putting curses on them, of making them sick, putting spells on them that spoil their food. Suspicion travels faster than sensibility and it spread across the ship faster than any disease born of the filth the slaves were made to live in; poor food, little exercise, the men spending most of their time laying head to toe with another slave only inches from each stinking body. The slavers had created their own curse, they just didn't know it.

Oh how Irisa wished she could use the darkness she knew she still had. At first she worried that it would stay in her homeland, that her gods would not travel with her. Fugra however had been adamant that Irisa had been born with a gift and it would be with her until her spirit returned to the gods. She would always have it, always need to control it. However for Irisa, the fact that she was were unable to save each slave that was raped, attacked, injured, either by slavers or one another, she worried that her power would wan. How could she still wield it when she had not been able to help these poor souls that would forevermore belong to the deep dark sea upon which they travelled upon.

It was after a full two weeks of daily torture

that finally Aleixo came to her during their exercise, she had given up hope that he had meant what he had said and she had sunk into a deep black mood, feeling betrayed by her Queen, her people and now Aleixo. Betrayal hurt and it fed those in the darkness.

He came bounding across the deck towards her, handsome in his uniform, albeit it being tattered and worn. They were still sailing in warm waters and the voyage so far had not been rough. Irisa did not notice him coming towards her, she was leaning over the deck watching a pod of dolphins dancing just off the ship's prow.She delighted in their sleek bodies, shining in the brilliant sunlight, sending sparkling diamonds skittering across the water as they sprayed the surface before splashing down deep into the dark waters again. For all the pain she felt herself smiling, this little family were happy and surviving and enjoying the cool deep water. She loved the sea, it reminded her of fishing trips with her mother from the small bay, of watching sunsets melt into the ocean like candles burning down in their holders.

Aleixo reached her and placed his hand lightly on her arm. She was startled and quickly turned to face him.

'Ah, it's you, you remembered that I was on the

ship with you then' she raised herself up, proud, adamant and full of anger with him, how dare he just appear with a smile as though nothing was wrong. She had trusted him and he had discarded her, left her when he promised he would not.What had she been thinking? Was she really stupid enough to have trusted the word of an Imbargala? It surprised her that this man, whom she didn't really know, who had been a lynch pin in stealing her and her fellow villagers away from their homes, this man, she had feelings for, she felt tender towards. It confused and frightened her and she could not think how to control those emotions, her soul resorting to anger.

Aleixo removed his hand and stared out to sea.

'I never forgot you for a moment Irisa, nor your friends, it takes time to get things done on the ship, I have some authority but I have to follow Vasconcelos's procedures or he would guess that I was trying to help slaves and then he would be angry beyond anything you have ever seen and no one would come off the better for it. I am regretful that you felt forgotten.'

He put his hand atop hers, holding the deck tightly, she did not gesture for him to move it this time and leant in towards his tall frame.

'I was scared Aleixo, have you seen what it is like for us? And we are lucky! Thank the Gods I am not a man! They are treated worse than the animals you keep, they at least can move away from one another.'

'I do not say I agree with what is happening on this ship Irisia and in front of you I am ashamed to say that if it were not for the desperate need for funds for my mother and sisters then I would not be here, but I am and I can't change that, what I can do is help those few that I have promised I will. I am allowed to have you as my slave now, it is all signed for, I own you now, so ...'

'Own me! You are no better than that bastard that stands preening and gloating at his hoard every day. I am not property, do you hear me? I am no one's property. I don't care what anyone says.'

'Oh you take me wrong again Irisa' Aleixo was exasperated at trying to explain. I have to 'own you' so I can protect you, when we get to the Americas you will be free to go. I have no wish to keep someone with me that does not want to be, it is the only way I could give you any protection on the ship. I have also persuaded the ship's surgeon to have Fugra as his assistant in the medical cabin. Amara is his slave, so I can protect all of you. If you don't want this, I will change those plans immediately.'

'No please, I am sorry. I know you do not think like those Imbargalas but it is hard to imagine why man would take other men to be slaves. I can not make sense of it in my head and it hurts that we must be given no choice. However I am grateful for your concern and I will be your slave and fulfil that however I must. I am grateful that you are helping my friends and I and I have seen you try to spread kindness to some other slaves. What do we do now?'

Aleixo smiled at her, 'Well now, you come to my cabin where you will stay with me. They think you will care for me, do my laundry, serve my wine and lay with me in my bed. For me, we are just sharing a cabin, I shall place no demands on you Irisa. Fugra and Amara will go to the surgeon's cabin. You will be given new clothes and more freedom and no more have to have that swill that they have been feeding you, it is no more than oats and milk, you must be famished.'

'We have survived,we know we are only fed and exercised like goats so we arrive in good condition. We won't though, the disease down there is rife. The captain needs to let Fugra, Amara and myself set up a regular cleaning routine with some of the other women and allow us to care for the sick, he will come off better for it, he'll have more slaves to sell when we reach whichever strange shore you are sailing to.'

'I will do what I can Irisa, come, let us go. I have clean warmed water so you can wash and dress.'

Irisa could not help but smile inwardly at the thought of clean water. She felt weighed down by filth and disease and needed to peel those layers off and strengthen herself if she was going to help others. At least she no longer had to worry about Fugra and Amara. It was with a slightly lighter heart that she left the deck than when she had entered it. She could hear the jeers behind them.

'Go on Aleixo! Go fuck her sideways!'

'Show us yer titties!'

' You gonna share her cunt then boy?'

'Watch out for that witch coven mate, she'll soon put a spell on yer dick!'

Irisa ignored the foul comments and the raucous laughter, she wasn't bothered what this group of pigs thought. Aleixo however could not contain his rage and turned to face the jeering sailors.

'I care not what you think, men. You will

however show me and my slave the respect due! I am your superior and unless you want to be flogged on deck you will keep your filth ridden paws off of her and stay away from me! Do you hear me, men?'

He did not have to repeat himself. The jeering died down, a few rumbles of 'aye aye sir' but most forced themselves to put their heads down and busy themselves with their work, aware of the position they would put themselves in if they upset the first mate. He had been a fair man and they didn't often get that, so they stopped the jeering, although behind closed doors when they bunked they still shared stories of what 'that witch' had done.

Chapter 19- Refuge.

Aleixo showed Irisa into a small but tidy cabin with a bed, shelves and a great chest under the bed for storage. There were candles and blankets and she felt at ease, comfortable, almost at home. He indicated the basin which was set up on a wooden unit with a jug underneath. On the bed lay a pile of underclothes and a dress with an apron and cap.

'I know this is not the dress of your homeland but it is clean. I'll leave you to wash and settle. When you're done why don't you lay on the bed and sleep for a while.' he smiled, turned and left her alone.

She had never felt so grateful to a person in her life. The warm water on her face felt luxurious after being caked in so much muck and filth. She grabbed a piece of muslin and began to scrub herself voraciously for the first time in weeks, the muslin cleaning off the worst of the filth. She rinsed and continued to wash until the water became dirtier than the cloth, then started to put on the clothes he had left. She had no idea what to do with them, especially the underclothes, they looked like thin, mens trousers, she presumed she had to put all of it on, she pulled them up over her legs and tied them at her waist, she then put on a linen slip, a rough cotton dress and apron to cover it. She left the cap, taking more of the muslim he had left and fashioned it into the headscarf she wore at home over her glorious black curls.

She felt a different person, a stranger to her own eyes, was this how she would be now? Dressed as the people in Aleixo's homeland.Would she still be Irisa? She felt like a bundle of cloth, would she really need to wear so much fabric when she got to the plantation, how would she work? She nervously brushed her fingers down over the fabric and lay upon the truckle bed. With its thin mattress and blankets, it was far from luxury but to Irisa who had so far only slept on the rough planks of the ship's carcass, without covers, it felt like she was lying on the softest sandiest shore, dozing in the sun, hearing the soft waves lap. The port hole in the room caught her eye and she delighted in discovering she could hear and see the sea, bobbing up and down as the ship moved through the waves, gradually the rhythmic movement and sound helped her drift off to sleep.

Amara and Fugra had been brought down further into the bowels of the ship, moving towards the rear where the surgeon had a small bay containing a grimy hammock, a table with a box for his tools, a shelf full of bottles that gave off a foul stench. The bay led to a cabin in the back with a small flat bed. Medical books filled the shelves, amongst which Amara was drawn to a beautiful painting full of sunlight and warmth over a landscape of rolling hills, the tallest, thickest trees she had ever seen, all leading down to a stream that in Amara's imagination was full of silvery fish.

For the first time, Evans' face lifted into the ghost of a smile, ' Ah I see you like the painting. This, ladies, is where the world is best! My beautiful England, I see those rolling hills from the window of my family residence every day and Lord how I miss them - he smiled wistfully into the air. He brought himself back to the moment with a jolt and indicated for the women to sit upon the truckle bed.

'So they tell me you know about medicine crones? I have known other savages such as yourselves who practise this and obviously it is inferior to my skills but I must admit I have seen some of it work. However I'll stand for none of your hoodooing, magic or dark matters that you all seem to be so fond of, do you hear me?

Amara quickly acquiesced, head down mumbling 'yes sir'

Fugra looked him square in the eyes 'My name is not Crone, it is Fugra, if you want me to help heal your sick and infected men, then that is what you will call me! I am a medicine woman as is Amara here and Irisa, who is with Aleixo. We use the roots and herbs of our homeland, that is not witchcraft you dim-witted turd!'

Evans took a step back, how dare this savage talk to him in such a way! Despite being incensed he had no idea of how to react to her outburst.

'Well, well, you will call me Sir or Mr Evans Sir!' he stuttered and stumbled over his words and Fugra struggled to contain her mirth at his reactions. 'We will indeed use your knowledge to heal the sick, you may treat the slaves you know to be ill or injured, we want good quality stock when we arrive back!'

He pointed at Fugra 'You Fugra, may go to the bay at the back, there is a mattress you can roll out onto the floor and that is where you will stay until it is time for you to fetch food or to check the sick as I command- do you understand, Fugra - Crone.'

Fugra got up and slowly walked towards him, 'Oh yes *sir*, I understand all too well and for the sake of my own people I will help to heal yours too, but do not underestimate us and what you call 'hoodooing' we know of darknesses that you can only dream of and you have angered our gods, they follow this ship and they will seek their vengeance, Mr Evans *sir!*'

Evans sighed with relief as she passed out of his sight, thank god she would be in the sick bay, she made him feel uncomfortable and he knew in his heart he could not control her, she did not succumb to the power or authority he held as an affluent white surgeon, he would do all he could to show her she must. In the meantime, this other slave seemed different, she was scared, he could feel it that meant he had the upper hand and could use it to his advantage. He gestured for Amara to lay down.

'You must be a tired young woman, I have seen how dark and dirty it is in that hold, foul fucking place, I don't see why I have to go down there to the sick, let them be brought to me!' He sat next to her on the bed and began stroking her hand. 'I can see you do not feel like the Crone, you have a gentle heart my dear, I think we are going to be friends.'

With that he began to lift the skirts Amara was now wearing and pushed himself down onto her, fumbling with his drawers.

'That's it my dear, let Evans do what he wanrs and I'll show you how kind I can be.'

Amara began to struggle, she tried to pull down her skirts to protect herself from the rape she knew was coming. His gentle facade broke as he began to get irritated with her.

'Lay still I say! You have been brought here for a purpose, now you will fucking fulfill it, open your legs now! You will be sorry if you do not!'

He slapped her hard around the face, Amara began to cry gently, but she no longer struggled, she lay as still as she could, trying to think of her home and the sea, the sound of the waves pounding against the ship as Evans pounded into her. With a grunt, he came inside her and wiped himself on her clothes.

'Get up! Now tidy this fucking cabin and I expect wine poured for me as I return, do you understand? Don't struggle next time and you may find I bring you back food from the Captains table, after a few weeks on this ship, you'll fuck anything just to eat, even me!'

He turned and left the cabin laughing to himself and his sickening humour. Amara pulled the fabric of the dress around her, curled into a ball and sobbed until she drifted off into a fitful doze.

Chapter 20- Creaking

Finally allowed on deck after weeks of being sequestered to the cabin for 'personal duties' , Amara sucked in the cool sea air with greed. Bruised, battered and covered in a thick woollen shawl that the 'darling' Mr. Evans had given her. He had made such a todo of it as he gave it to her, with that fake smile and equally fake words. The weeks in the cabin had led her to learn that Evans had minimal medical knowledge, cared not a jot for any human life bar his own and was only interested in making money and getting off the ship in order to gamble more.

He spent most of the time drinking the foul stenching wine, ending up out of his cups, which more often than not led to him becoming violent during the sexual acts he made her perform for him, always when he had sent Fugra away. She seethed with hatred for him and for shame at what she had let her body do for him. She saw Irisa across the deck and slowly made her way to her.

Irisa began to talk, bubbly and bright, Amara gave a tired smile, Irisa looked more closely and gasped, ' Amara, what has happened to your face?'

'Well, Mr. Evans will tell you I am clumsy and

fall often when the ship sways, truth be told Irisa, he is careless with his hands, his fists and anything he can pick up and beat me with before he rapes me, I am ashamed to tell you all that he does, of course it is all ok, I am a slave and this is my purpose apparently.

Irisa drew her friend close to her and held her tight. 'I am so sorry Amara, I had no idea, I have seen Fugra and although she calls him a snake, she gave no indication that you were being abused in this way.'

Amara sighed, 'Oh he doesn't do this to Fugra or while she is around, he's scared witless of her (she gave a soft laugh and grabbed her ribs)Just like when we were children, he is convinced she is a witch and will curse him if he does anything to her, he makes her stay with the sick or injured in the medicine room. I have to stay in the cabin, waiting for when he comes in and wants me in some sick or perverted way. I am ruined, Irisa, my life is over, I should have stayed with Magra!'

Thick, hot tears fell across Amaras bruised and swollen face. Irisa let them fall as Amara's body softly jerked whilst she sobbed and released the floodgate of emotion she'd desperately been trying to hold in, they burst forth like a river bank in the rainy season and she allowed herself to be swallowed in the misery feeling safe with her only true friend she had who could understand. As Amara prepared to go back below deck, wiping her eyes so the vile man could not see how he had made her feel, Irisa stroked her face and pulled the cloak close around her friend.

'Amara. Listen, we need to meet; me, you, Fugra. I will ask Aleixo for help, when we meet I will raise the darkness, we will end that vile man, we will send him the ones waiting for vengeance. They are strong now, I am stronger now. I can feel them within me, swirling, waiting, sensing, biding their time. I can't do that on my own. I don't want to implement Aleixo in this, I know he is an Imbargala, but he has been nothing but a kind and gentle man since he owned me. I won't see him punished for my actions but keep strong little one, I will help you, he won't do this again.'

Amara nodded in acceptance, too hurt, angry and debased to argue that the darkness should stay in the dark as she had before but it was either this or she took her own life, she couldn't take any more. She moved away from Irisa as they were guided onside with the rough use of ropes, gropes, slaps, just another day on board the grand Juniper!

Back in Aleixo's cabin Irisa lit the lamps as the chill night mist swirled around the ship. She prepared wine and food for him, tidied herself and sat on the bed, planning and plotting, thinking. Her head was so conflicted and filled with images of her dear friend who had been horrifically abused. Oh it wasn't something new on the ship, women were raped and abused all the time, along with many of the male slaves and some of the lower, younger mariners. Several had taken exercise on deck as an opportunity to throw themselves to the anticipative sharks rather than be ripped apart on their floating hell. However this was different, this was personal, family, she could not let this go, she just wasn't sure how to approach the matter with Aleixo. She lay back on the thick cotton covers and listened, she listened to the roar of the waves as the ship ploughed through their peaks and troughs, almost thrown into the air and caught again by the white foamy waves, she listened to the ship, she could hear it's speech, it's sorrow, it's creaks and clicks as the wood swelled and shrunk with the wet and the heat as the men moved about on deck, as it shouted to the waves; 'no! Enough now!' then fell silent as they fell into the doldrums and a still plateaux of water.

What would this ship be able to tell her children, her grandchildren, would it tell the tale of the deck with the rough sailors and the Imbargalas, the salty air and freedom, or would it tell the story of those trapped below deck, chained and humiliated, wishing for something to speed them away to death rather than live another minute as a belonging with no more than a tot of port. Waves lapped, wood creaked and slowly she drifted away into her mind, into her thoughts and into her plans, so that by the time she was startled back to being fully awake as Aleixo came into the cabin, she had fully made up her mind to tell him everything, yes, everything.Then, she thought, let us see if he still stands by me as he claims he will or would she be the next one given to the mariners for sport until bloodied and sullied, she be tossed overboard, too damaged to sell but her soul saved by being returned to the sea she loved.

Aleixo slumped down on the low bed, sighing. 'I am so tired Irisa, I wish we were nearer the Americas, we only have a few more weeks on this ship but it feels like a lifetime, so many are sick and dying, I can't seem to see what to do to make a difference.'

She passed him a cup of porto and gently caressed the side of his face. 'I am sorry things are not good for you, please understand for my people this is a slow death, we would rather be with our ancestors than on this damn ship!'

Gently Aleixo placed his hand on top of hers. 'I'm sorry Irisa, I sometimes forget now that you are with me, what is actually happening below decks. I wish I had a way to stop it all but I don't.'

She knelt down in front of him and laid her head in his lap. He gently unwound the scarf from her tight glossy curls and pulled his fingers through their ringlets and twirls.

Hesitantly Irisa began to share her innermost secrets with him and what was happening to Amara. She had hidden these secrets so well, it was a difficult thing to bring them out into the open now. She was so nervous of his reaction, she had grown fond of him and she didn't want him to let her go and choose another. She worried about her God's reactions, would they allow her to voice her gifts to this man with no beliefs in her world?

'Aleixo, I can help, I can help those below, I can help the sick, I can help my friend but you will have to trust me and take a leap of faith that I am not sure you are ready for, this will not be easy for you to hear but I know of no other way.'

He smiled warmly and turned her chin so he could look deeply into her eyes, those beautiful brown/black pools of light. 'There is nothing you can say that will push me away, speak freely.'

'I will not hold you to that, just listen to the end if you can, please.'

So, Irisa started at the beginning, she told him of her father, how the darkness lept from her, how Fugra and Amara had helped, how she had got rid of the evil in her village. She explained her plan to rid the ship of its surgeon and why, allowing for Fugra to take charge of the sick with her herbs and potions along with Irisa and Amara, knowing that no longer would her friend be treated like a rag and thrown away when she was used.

Aleixo was silent as she told her tale of Gods of old, from her homeland, how they had followed the ship, how she could feel them and how with help she could use them. A silence seemed to stretch before them into an eternity, which he finally broke;

'So you *are* witches then?'

'No Aleixo! Have you not listened to anything I've said? I was given a gift from our Gods, the rest of what we do is from our knowledge of herbs and plants, passed on from mother to daughter, I am no witch!'

'I'm sorry, I just can't seem to find the words. It is unbelievable, not that I don't believe you or in you.'

'So, what is your decision? I understand if you wish me to go.'

She stood up and turned away. He moved towards her quickly, grabbing onto her hand, turning her to face him in an embrace that promised more. 'I will stand by you until the day I die. Evans is a sick entitled man who does nothing to help my men or your people, his pride keeps him from allowing you to help, we'll be better off without him. If I could get away with sticking a knife in his stomach I would! It makes me sick to think what he is doing to Amara, that he believes this is how to treat any human being, any woman is vile beyond belief.'

He kissed her then, warm, soft, needful and she reciprocated with a heat she'd not felt before. He pulled her to the bed and together they discovered each other in new ways until exhausted, they slept entangled on the tiny bed among limbs, sheets and sweat.

Chapter 21- The Darkness awakes.

Irisa awoke, still drowsy to a noise she was not sure she had imagined. She'd not heard it since leaving her coastal home and part of her wasn't sure if she had dreamt it, but then, she heard it again, the keening of birds, birds that lived at sea but were bound for home to nest and mate. Gulls! Land was near! She sat up in bed with a heart that felt lighter than since leaving Allada. On deck the Mariners seemed as though they were scrambling, shouting, pulling on ropes, hauling sails to take advantage of the breeze. She could hear the birds clearly now, their raucous voices were calling home to their soul mates. She saw Aleixo talking to the men and held back until he had finished, once he had dismissed them, she caught his attention and waved, he strode over to her.

'The Gulls! Are we near land? Finally? After all these weeks!'

'Yes, we are finally close to the Americas, we are still a couple of weeks away from land but we are heading in the right direction, finally from there to my homeland will be able to call me, just as this birdsong calls to you.'

Irisa didn't want to think about what would happen after Aleixo left her at the plantation, they hadn't discussed that yet, both too afraid to to face the truth of the matter.

'Irisa, if we are going to do something about Evans, we need to do it soon.'

She nodded, walking away, 'I will talk to Amara and Fugra today.'

Although anxious for their own safety amongst the many calls of 'witch' they gathered daily from the crew, the three wise women knew instinctively what they needed to do. They had schemed and planned together with determination to end the dark and sadistic personality of Mr. Evans, Sir!. They knew all they now needed was to wait until the dear Mr. Evans had been drinking- which he did on a nightly basis and when he was oblivious to the world around him, Irisa would call the darkness. When it was over, Fugra and Amara would say they were healing the sick, Aleixo would attest that he had seen Evans out of his cups swaying aboard deck, leading the crew to believe he had fallen overboard, it was a plausible hazard on board ship, especially with a man that had never gained his sea legs, no one would miss the harsh, self-entitled pompous idiot.

The following night as the gulls finished their caterwauling, Evans began his nightly drunken stupor, falling down beneath the hammock in his bay. With fewer crew on deck this time of night, Irisa, Fugra and Amara persuaded the drunken letch up onto the deck, Fugra strongly advising he take the air to help with his sickness from the drink. They then hid in one of the small boats they carried, under a thick tarpaulin so no one would see what happened when Irisa called the darkness.

Fugra gave a solemn smile, 'find them quickly girl, hold onto that darkness, don't let yourself become lost in it, we need you here, now start this.'

Squashed into the small boat, Irisa knelt in front of Evans unconscious, snoring body, she closed her eyes. Amara reached across and grabbed her hand, whilst Fugra placed a grounding hand upon the top of her head and she began, She felt herself slide into the blackness, it was cold, harsh, hostile. They were angry they had been suppressed, the Gods should not be denied, Durnos and his minions seethed,they could sense the evil on the ship, black, white and all in between and they were ravenous for them. Irisa held firm, controlling the swirling, engorged mass of black shadowy tendrils moving their way through her body, she gagged as her mouth opened and continued beyond the natural until it became an unearthly maw. She made a sound that none that heard it that night would ever forget, the superstitious mariners claiming they had heard a banshee and that it heralded back luck or death, others claimed it was a mermaid singing, no the mermaids of children's folklore and fairy tales, evil sirens, sea sprites who would drag you to the bottom of the ocean to a swift and painful death.

The tendrils began to thicken and pull themselves from Irisa, winding and tightening over Evans body. He opened his eyes in blank terror, black pupils dilated with fear, he had no time to voice his indignation, or to question what he saw because before he could blink, he was gone, left this world and left not one grieving soul behind him. Irisa slumped forward, Fugra caught her gently and folded her into her arms. Amara's face was lined with tears, tears of gratitude for the loss of the evil presence Evans created and for the safe return of her friend from whatever realm she went into when these strange incidents occurred.

Fugra, ever practical, was trying to push the girls from the boat and forward onto the ship before they were caught. Irisa felt empty, she knew without a doubt she had been given no choice but to act, there was no one else who could have stopped him, but still, ending another's life was not something she did lightly and she felt the pain of the man who had been formed into the monster he became by the way he had been treated in life, she only hoped that in death he would find peace and knew that his family would find happiness again without his continuous debasement.

Aleixo had watched from a distance, he had been both fascinated and horrified by what he had been told and although he wanted to believe them, he still had doubts as to whether something so extraordinary could be true. However, now he could not unsee what he had witnessed and he was shocked that something as violent as ending a life could make your soul feel lighter and relieved. He worried about Irisa and wanted them all out as quickly as possible, what he'd witnessed would undoubtedly be classed as 'magicks by blacks' . Rumours of being a witch meant risking death, for all of them.

He moved forward crouching low, hiding from the bright moonlight that had been hiding behind thick woolly night clouds and was now daring the world to believe it was daylight.

He knocked on the edge of the boat, whispering 'it's me, quickly come this way, I can get you back to your rooms without notice.'

They followed meekly, grateful he had come to aid them, holding on to each other, only now allowing fear to brew in their minds. There needed to be no doubt about where they were that night. Thankfully months on the ship meant Aleixo could guide them in almost blinding blackness once they left the deck and within minutes they were all back in their rooms completing their usual nightly tasks, although each slept fitfully that night each probing their own conscience.

The following morning Fugra went to Vasconcelos and informed him that the surgeon had not come back to the sick bay the night before, that he had left sick patients waiting for their medicines and that she knew not where to find him. She hinted heavily that she suspected him laid up drunk , the Captain raised his eyebrows in response.

'Mmm, well if he is not found by eventide then we will start searching for him, how can he be missing on a ship for the Lord's sake! Maybe he's fallen and knocked himself out whilst administering medicines, he's a bloody liability that man, wish I'd never brought him! Now leave off your whining Crone and cease to bother me.'

She scuttled away from his ire, smirking to herself as she went, of course Evans did not appear at sunset and as dusk began to envelop the ship lanterns were lit and the crew half heartedly began wandering the creaking vessel, calling his name without response. No one on that ship was truly keen to find the cure. As the fog moved in and threatened to end the search, Aleixo shouted to the gang and held up the doctor's bag, filled with bottles of porto, which had been left by the edge of the deck. As planned the Captain and his crew came to the conclusion that the dullard had been drunk and had fallen overboard, that there was no hope now of recovering him and that the sharks would have rapaciously pulled him apart beneath the dark blue swirling waters that held aloft their ship.

And as easily as that, another human life was written off.

The following morning there was no sign of the previous night's trauma or weather for that matter. The sky was cerulean and grand with pink wisps and white cotton clouds giving it a dappled effect. Irisa awoke in Alcixo's arms, she lay still and silent and there it was again! The call of the gulls, louder today, she could hear the expectation in their calls, they were going home, they were going home! However calm and contented Irisa felt, she could still sense a tension in the air. She turned from Aleixo's warmth, would this be it now? Had he finally realised that her gift made her evil and that he would have no part of it in this world or the next. These were not his gods after all.

Aleixo was laying on his back staring at the ceiling, a frown set hard across his tanned forehead. Gently Irisa touched his arm and he turned to face her.

'Aleixo do you want me to leave? I understand it is hard for you, for me, my people are grateful for any gift we are given from our Gods, for me it is this power, for others like Fugra it is her ability to heal those who would otherwise not survive. Evans was a cruel, sadistic man, head terrors in his head that disturbed me to know, we are protecting many others by ending him;men, women, even children, he had lusts that no creature on earth should possess.

ALeixo stared straight into her eyes. ' I know all

that is true, part of me is in awe of you, that you have this, this gift. I admire that you only use it when there are others who have been or will be harmed in the cruellest of ways, it is incredible! Fantastical! But it scares me, scares me that someone who appears so vulnerable can hold such power, that it might overtake you, that I may lose you to whatever this is.'

He stroked her soft face with his rough fingers. 'It is not my conscience Irisa, that is quite clear, that man, that animal was a self-entitled pig! But you, I couldn't bear to lose you.'

Irisa's salty tears fell gently onto the pillow.

'Oh Irisa, I didn't want to upset you, I just don't want there to be any secrets between us, or things left unsaid. I want you to know how I feel and for you to be honest with me, that is all.

Irisa wiped her eyes and gave a weak smile. 'I am not distressed by what you said Aleixo, I am grateful for your honesty, I simply thought you hated me for what I am, I didn't realise it was concern not hatred.'

Aleixo gave a short laugh ' How could I ever hate you, since meeting you, I have found the truth inside me and who I am, I can't begin to think of a life without you.'

Irisa sat up hugging her knees close to her chin.

'You are going to have to, if we are soon to be at this plantation, we don't have much time left, people like us do not mix, it is wrong, we have been lucky to find this time on the Juniper but I am not naive enough to believe that 'we' can exist outside of it's timbers.'

Aleixo frowned ' The plantation? What are you? My Lord you don't truly think that after all this I am going to leave you there to work your body and soul into the ground! How could you even have that thought in your head, Irisa?'

He turned from her, feeling spurned.

'Well I just assumed that would happen, let's not pretend that it won't be happening with my fellow villagers, I know that the slaves are sold at market, I just presumed I would be one of them.'

There was a wall between them now, as real as any they could have built with dense clay or mud bricks, both drowned in hurt and fear for each other's voiced thoughts, not realising the hurt that lay beneath their spoken words.

Aleixo turned to face Irisa, gently lifting her head from her knees to face him.

'When I said I owned you and you were angry, I

explained then that I wanted to save you, you know I don’t believe in slavery, that for me this trip is a means to an end and that I will have to have that on my conscience for the rest of my life, but because of this voyage, my family won't starve and I have found a woman I love and Irisa I do love you, however wrong it is. I thought you would accompany me on my return trip to Europe, to Portugal, I thought you would come home with me.’

Irisa’s tears became sobs, catching in her throat, she struggled to get her voice to work, her thoughts unable to create the words she wanted and needed to say. She reached out to Aleixo and he pulled her close.

‘I had no idea you felt that way, I just presumed what would become of us, but you are being naive, you seem to be overlooking the fact that I am a black woman, thought of as worthless slave, I’m now a nothing, how could you think of taking me to your home, you would be ruined, your mother would disown you, I could not do that to you Aleixo because despite the fact that you and your men have ripped my family and friends from their homes, despite the fact that you and your men have abused and controlled us, I fond I love you too, I have prayed to the Gods to change this, to stop this but I can't and for all the salt in the sea, I would not hurt you.'

Aleixo pulled her to him, crushing her frail body against his, stroking her hair as her sobs eased.

'Well that was a hell of a way to declare our love for one another!' he started to laugh, gently at first, then deeper, panting guffaws leaving his lips.

Irisa wiped her hand across her face, wiping away the tears. She looked into his eyes, this man meant what he said, she could feel it, she could sense his gentleness, fairness, empathy pouring from his soul. Aleixo's breathing slowed and calmed along with Irisa's. They could feel each other's heart beats, beating in unison now as one.

'My mother would welcome you into our home with all her heart. We do not hold with slavery in our village, in fact black people from Amsterdam have travelled to our shores, they do not hold with putting one man above another or a woman below, a man. Yes there are politics, there are still rich and poor but should you want it, there is a home for you and we will find a way to get there. When we land, I will declare my intention to keep you and not sell you, that is a right that comes with my position thank goodness. Then we will find a way to get you back on that ship and back to my home, I promise you.

Irisa stared into the close musty air of the room, the sun's heat beginning to share its warmth with those on the ship.

‘What about my friends, what will happen to Fugra and Amara now? I don’t know if I can watch them be dragged onto the plantation whilst I wander off into the sunset, they are my family Aleixo.’

He nodded solemnly, ‘I don’t know what will happen to them now. It could be that the Captain will claim them for himself as Evans has been declared dead, he could choose to sell them, yes, but we may be able to come up with a plan where they come with us. I will try everything for you, but in the end it is not something I can swear to Irisa, I wish I could.’

Irisa left the bed and walked to the small porthole, looking out to sea.

‘We belong to the sea, our kind, you feel it too don’t you, I can sense it. Our souls feel the tug of the waves, the salt in its spray, the raw power and the energy it wields. The sounds lull us to sleep at the end of the day and the crashing waves wake us as a new day is formed, we all belong to the sea and I fear that if we can not save Fugra and Amara, I would rather fill the water cover my mouth, fill my lungs and drag me below.'

'Please Irisa, you are distressing me now. I will do all I can to save them but for me, I have to put you above them, that's where my heart is, you have to come first.'

Irisa shivered as she shook the gloominess from her shoulders and her heart.

'I understand Aleixo, for now let us enjoy the time we have left. I would like to help Fugra and Amara to check on all the slaves that have survived, try to treat those who are still suffering, could that be arranged?'

'I will ask Vasconcelos this morning, I will also try to find out his plans for your friends.'

Irisa moved to the wash basin and splashed water over her face. She had just spent the most fractious, frightening moment on the ship so far and it had shook her to the core. She needed time to clear her head, to be still, to calm her thoughts. Once Aleixo had dressed and left the cabin, she followed and swiftly made her way to Fugra, she needed her skills and reassurance.

Chapter 22- Changes

Fugra had moved into Evans cabin with Amara the previous night as soon as the crew understood Evans was dead. They had shared the truckle bed for the night and both had slept soundly for the first time since boarding the ship. Amara had felt no fear, knowing Evans would not use her again and with Fugra there to look after her, she felt safe, protected and slept deeply. Fugra had the joy of not sleeping on the floor with a rag, instead laying on a mattress with cotton covers. Comfort gave her the rest she needed. The sense of relief she had that both of 'her girls' now would be safe was a huge weight lifted from her and she felt that she could face whatever would become of them next.

Amara did not wake at the soft rap on the cabin door, too deep in her slumber. Fugra did, leaving the warmth and comfort of the bed somewhat reluctantly, she made her way to the door.

'Who is it? Whose bloody sick now?' she shouted to the wooden divide, she would only open it if she had to, however safe she felt they were still only two women alone with no protection.

'It's me, Irisa, I need to speak with you.'

'Wait child, I will come to you, let Amara rest, it has been a long while since she has been allowed untroubled sleep.'

Fugra threw on a thick hessian dress over her tunic, wrapped a shawl around her shoulders and opened the cabin door gently.

'Come child, let us talk on deck, we will be undisturbed there.'

They clambered their way over the sleeping night crew, the day watch was in control now and they would be too busy to mind an old Crone and her negress witch friend. Irisa followed Fugra as she shuffled towards the prow of the ship, sitting on the rough planks in a spot where none would spy. She bade Irisa sit.

'Come now child, unburden yourself, there's usually a reason you come to me.'

Irisa sighed 'I don't know where to start.'

'Oh come now! I don't give a rat's arse where you start, just say what you came to say.'

Irisa fidgetted and tried several times to start her tale but every time the words left her, they were muddled or made no sense, she looked despairingly at Fugra who produced some Intsenga leaves from her pocket.

‘For Durnos sake, it’ll be dark again before you’re done. Evans may no longer roam this plane but there are others who will be watching and I have people to help, come on, chew the leaves, calm, then unburden yourself.’

As Irisa began to chew lightly on the dark sickly green leaves, she began to feel her body relax, she felt her tongue tied mind loosen and she began to tell Fugra what had happened with Aleixo, what she thought would happen and her fear of losing either her lover or her family.

Fugra chuckled gently, ‘Oh Irisa! Can you surely have turned into such a dreamer, did you really think that we would all survive this hellish trip? We have all faced death in the eye at some point and won, is that still not enough for you? You thought we would all walk off this ship and carry on with life, as healthy as when we were stolen and shoved onto the thing!’

Fugra’s tone changed, Irisa felt her anger and frustration streaming towards her.

‘Look around you girl, people are dying! Our people, their people, all dying! We are rife with disease, hunger, despair, friends have been raped and tortured, force fed with metal instruments they call a ‘speculum oris’, a grand name for a shiny piece of metal, have you seen them force feed those that would rather starve to death? Shoving it down their gullets, making them heave, bleed and Durnos knows what else, just so they can force that fucking gruel down a neck so they don't loose a coin when we reach wherever this damn ship is taking us! And all the while, these 'ghaboun,'these stupid rat Imbargalas keep coming at us, it is endless Irisa. If Aleixo can get you out of this danger and get you to a safe place then I can die a happy old woman. I'll pray to Gynos and call down a storm to take me right now if it means that just one of you can be safe, maybe not even free but safe.'

Fugra hurriedly wiped the tears that had left her eyes, mumbling curses at the salty air for making them leak.

Irisa leant against the old woman, who softened and held out her hand.

'You are like my mother, I don't think I could go on without you.'

'And you, you are like my daughter and my heart is full for you, but you can and must go on, do it for every one of us who cannot.'

They stole a few moments together just to sit and be, to take in the moment, for Irisa to accept that as a chosen slave she had weathered this journey in a way those crammed down in the hold could not, even the sailors had a harder journey, working incessantly in all weathers, she accepted without guilt that she had been lucky and that she could not save everyone. Their amiable silence was ruined by Pero who was scrubbing the decks.

'Ah, witches,' he smirked. 'And what are you conspiring today you filthy whores? How to unman us, how to kill us? I still don't believe you didn't have anything to do with the missing doctor, strange that he had you two for company and now he's shark feed! I will find out what you are planning and I will have you burnt! You sicken me.'

Irisia sighed 'Oh Pero, the only one with a sickness is you, it pours from your heart like sand on the shore, we are not your enemy, we are not your curse, grieve and let them go Pero, your sister and your mother do not want this to be the way you live.'

Irisa moved to get up from the deck, Pero pushed her down, pressing hard onto her stomach with his foot.

'Shut up! Shut Up! Shut the fuck up!' he screamed 'You have no right to even think about my mother and sister, if it weren't for black bastards like you, they would still be here and maybe I would not be so damn bitter! But they are dead and so I am. I watched while men like your villagers fucked them until they bled before killing them. You're fucking animals!'

He spat on her face and removed his foot.

Irisa wiped the sticky mucus from her cheek and sat up.

'You're right Pero, they were animals, but they were not my people, they came from far away lands that I never knew existed until Aleixo told me what had happened to him as a child. They came to raid, rape and steal slaves, you are doing the same thing to us now! How can you bear it? You know the cost of this. I am sorry for you Pero, I truly am.'

Pero looked away wounded by her words, the truth of them hitting him like an arrow.

'I don't want your fucking pity whore, go back to your cabin and moan to my slave loving friend. We all know you have him under a spell.'

Irisa leant down and helped Fugra to her feet, she rushed at Pero, her hands flying like claws trying to wound him.

'Get off you fucking witch! You're mad! I will have you burned I swear it!'

Irisa put her hand on Fugra, 'Please stop this Fugra, he is damaged, he doesn't wound me or scare me, he is weak.'

Fugra prodded him in the chest with a gnarled finger, 'The Gods are watching, they will avenge us, Takhir will find you and you will know pain.'

Pero laughed into her face, 'Let's see who burns first then, witch!' he stomped away muttering to himself, his rage burning in his chest like a hot stone in a fire.

Irisa put her arm through Fugras' ' Come Fugra, let's make some more pasta with the last of the centrella, he can do us no harm.'

'Mmm, well he's a snake and I don't trust him.'

Irisa smiled at her and they walked back along the deck, back down to the cabins, as they came to the barricade, the barrier separating the men and women on deck, Aleixo came running out.

'Irisa, Fugra Are you well? Did the bastard Pero hurt you? I'll have him punished.'

Irisa looked at him quizzically, 'How did you know Pero had found us?'

'One of the young deckhands, he'd been in the crows nest and heard the commotion, he came to find me when he saw you were in trouble, he knows you are mine and that I am fond of you.'

Fugra laughed, ' That is what you young folk call it now is it? How many times a night are you fond of her Aleixo?'

Irisa frowned at Fugra, ' That is quite enough thank you, you know we care for one another.'

Aleixo made his way to the pair and manoeuvred himself between them, helping Fugra walk back to the cabin; he could sense that despite her outward stance, she had been shocked by Pero's behaviour.

'Come.' he said 'Vasconcelos is looking for you, he wants me to bring you and Amara to his cabin. I know not whether he intends to sell you, gift you to another or to keep you but I have tried to make him see your usefulness and that will stand you in good stead with him. More use, more money sadly.'

Fugra huffed but continued walking.

'Well let's go, I can't wait to see what the Gods have in store for us next boy!'

'I'll go and collect Amara, you can either come with me or go make your way to his cabin.'

Irisa thought for a moment, 'we'll stay together, it's safer that way, come Fugra.'

Fugra began mumbling about scrambling over

the whole bloody ship to find the man but had enough sense to keep her voice low.

'Irisa, you had better go to my cabin, there is no need to make him aware of you yet, it is Fugra and Amara he wants to see.

Irisa nodded, 'please take care of them both Aleixo.'

Vasconcelos gave a gruff command to enter the cabin when they reached it. His head was poured over thick vellum charts and maps laid out on a heavy wooden table, he was drinking from a large cup of wine, mumbling to himself, marking the vellum with a large quilled ink pen.

Despite their presence he continued with his annotation of the maps. Aleixo coughed gently,

'Sir, I have brought the slaves that Mr. Evans owned. Remember I mentioned them to you sir, they are proficient with the use of herbs, many of our own men are alive because of them.'

Vasconcelos looked up and gently placed his cup down.

'Ah yes, well bring them in, I need to see them. I have taken account of what you said but if I listen to all the mariners, they are witches are they not?'

Fugra took a step forward despite Aleixo trying

to hold her back.

'We are no witches, Captain! We work with herbs and make medicines and sometimes luck, there is no witchcraft in that!'

'Mmm, quite.' he smirked at them 'well, I think it's an intriguing possibility. I think that until we reach the plantation, you will belong to yourself. However, if you are willing to help with the medical care of the men, you might well put yourselves in a better position when we land, what say you?'

Amara and Fugra looked at one another and then voiced their agreement.

'Good, excellent, now you will sleep in the surgeon's cabin together, from tomorrow morning I will expect you to make daily rounds of any of the men who are sick, do you understand?'

Fugra bowed her head, ' Yes sir, we thank you for your kindness and we will do whatever we can.'

He dismissed them with a wave of his hand. Aleixo escorted them back to their cabin.

'You will be safe here, make sure at night you lock yourselves in, Fugra please no funny business, if you comply it will be better for you and Amara when we reach land, it is the most I can do for you, please for the sake of Amara and Irisa, do not make war with

Vasconcelos, I beg of you.'

Fugra snorted, 'You do not need to beg me, son, I am not an idiot. This bodes well for us and we thank you for your voice. Now go and do your job so we can actually arrive at land, I've had enough of this fucking water now.'

Aleixo laughed to himself as he walked away, satisfied that in the circumstances he had helped Irisa's friends as best he could.

Chapter 23 - Bird call.

The following weeks were hard. Irisa had become impatient to land once she had heard the gulls calling, hoping each day she would hear the lad in the crows nest bark out 'ahoy! Land ahoy!' Life during the day aboard the Juniper was hard, little food or fresh water, the fresh water bitterly rationed as they were towards their journey's end and no rain fell for them to catch the thirst quenching blobs. She often thought, as her stomach cramped for food and her throat ached for water how much better off she still was than those imprisoned in the hold. The heat had returned as they neared land and the bowels of the ship were stifling, the scent, stomach churning. With the support of the Captain making it clear that Amara and Fugra belonged to him, they were relatively unmolested and many of the men allowed themselves to be treated. They had come to rely on the women in the past weeks and were more pleasant in their company. All in all it was difficult but bearable.

Then three weeks after Irisa had first heard those argumentative gulls, she heard the calls of other birds, birds she did not recognise, then came that moment that they had all been praying for for months, the sound of ‘Land Ahoy!’ There was much cheering and clambering on the ship, everyone had scrambled out to see what the fuss was about and now the mariners, Imbargalas and slaves who were on deck exercising were all cheering, even Vasconcelos was cheerful for once.

"We have finally reached our journey men, those of us left have earnt the right to rest on these islands and will be enjoying wine, women and song within the week! For now though, we have our final job with these savages, bring them up, they need cleaning and oiling ready for market, as they are, they'll just repulse the slave merchants, let's make our coin men!’

The noise was deafening, Irisa was grateful for surviving the voyage but dreading the moment when she would have to watch her fellow villagers being sold like fish on the market.

Irisa, Fugra and Amara were put with the Imbargalas so that as the slaves were brought up, splashed with sea water and then oiled to highlight their dark skin and strong muscles- their usefulness, they could also be checked for disease or injury and treated if possible. Fugra struggled to contain her ire, she understood these poor wretches were only being given the comfort of clean water and treatment so that they fetched a higher price when they were thoughtlessly sold and it caught in her throat that she was part of it, but what choice did she have? If she refused she'd be one of the starved, stinking slaves herself, then who could she help? No, as much as it caused anger and hurt in her heart, she would treat those she could and hope that they moved on to at least humane owners, who would equally keep them fit and alive, even if that was so they had a good worker, for many it was the best outcome she could wish them. The more useful she and the girls could be, the more chance they too would find a better place.

Irisa applied poultices to infected wounds, washing them out as gently as she could with sea water and dirty rags. Amara was given the job of oiling her people, until they gleamed in the sun.Apparently this made her kind more attractive to the British and American owners who would buy them to use them how they wished. How strange these people were. Amara felt uncomfortable and confused at what the strange white folk thought was proper. The process took days but by the end of it, the group of survivors looked more human than they had for the majority of the trip and were deemed ready by Vasconcelos. An ominous air infiltrated the slave deck, the stolen felt their anxiety grow

Chapter 24- Arrival

The following day, Vasconcelos called for the ship to be anchored in a small bay in a place Irisa heard Aleixo call Virginia. The deck was like a beehive, everybody had a purpose but an observer would see only chaos. Men were running hither and thither, pulling and securing ropes, preparing the small boats for crossing to the shore.

Pero was in charge of the slaves as they were herded onto the deck in preparation for the crossing. The fittest and healthiest of the slaves first, down to the poor souls who were last to leave, bones protruding through their rough hemp shifts, eyes sunken, hearts and heads broken with death and disease.

Irisa watched on, lucky to be accompanying Aleixo, who at that moment was serving Vasconcelos on the top deck. She was sickened by the sight of the pompous man, dressed as though on the way to a royal court, not about to sell a human cargo, just as he would rum. Irisa knew What the fates held for her fellow villages, they would be sold into slavery, for Life, they would be working the newly planted tobacco plantations until they dropped with exhaustion, their days running into one another until they either survived and continued with the endless monotony or died and passed to the gods for rest.

‘ Look at them Aleixo! see we have produced some fine slaves for the market! the traders will be paying top coin for ours they need many for this year many died last year during their seasoning.’

‘ seasoning sir?’ asked Aleixo curiously

‘ Yes man, seasoning, the first year they're here they either get used to the heat and work or they die from what I've heard they even had some die while holding the Damn hoes! Ha! Well all the better for us I say! You ready boy?’

Aleixo Could sense Irisa’s eyes burning into his back, feeling her resentment at his apparent acceptance of how amusing Vasconcelos seemed to find the deaths of Slaves, how they could be forgotten and replaced so easily. He lowered his head.

‘Yes sir, of course for Sir, it's been a long time since I sailed home and home is what I'm aching for. Are you not missing London and home? Family?’

He had hoped to show Irisa but there was more to the man than what he knew she could see, he was quickly disappointed.

'Home! Good God no! back to my moaning wife and three daughters, they are a drain on my soul and my purse! unless God has intervened and my inadequate wife has finally managed to arrange marriages for my daughters whilst we've been away! be glad to get back to the boys club though being served the finest brandy and cigars while sharing tales of our adventures, those old bastards lap it up, they'll have some fine fillies ready for us too I'll warrant.'

Irisa Sighed deeply and looked away, to the dock, little more than a few strips of wood on the shore for the Gentry to stand on-god forbid they wet those leather boots they all wore. She watched with an ache in her belly as the slaves made their way further onto the beach where a group of white men dressed like Vasconcelos stood, holding Canes, laughing and taking no regard for the human tragedy that was before them.

'Come Aleixo, we have the boat for ourselves and our slaves, let's get off this damn ship and find us some adventures worth sharing back home!' He gave Aleixo a thump on the back and began making his way to the final boat, briefly glancing back to make sure Alexa was following.

Irisa felt shadow circling her soul her mind and knew that she was struggling to contain the monstrous power within her, so much pain and resentment, but she had to survive, she had to find a way to protect her friend and though she loved, Aleixo, Amara and Fugura.

She turned her head to Aleixo, ‘I love you Aleixo, With all my heart and without you I doubt I would have survived this trip, but hear me well, I can't let these people be harmed, abused, I need to save them Aleixo, even if that means we do not make it home, I owe them that at least.’

Aleixo frowned and for the first time she saw a temper lying beneath his gentle exterior.

‘For God's sake Irisa! I have done all I can to protect you to keep your friends safe. I have told you I have to get home, I too have responsibilities! Yes this is a situation I hoped never to be in, but even with all the power from your gods, you could not save all of your people, we need to focus on us and your friends, that is realistic. If you use your power here and now, people will see, that could not be avoided if done in plain sight, if you plan to end or torture so many souls, they will burn you as a witch, there is no happy ending Irisa, we just have to make the best one that we can. Now come, because without you there is no life for me, please irisa.'

Tears fell gently down her soft shining skin and glinted as they hit the worn deck ' I know that in my heart but I am so angry, I can feel it coursing through me, Aleixo and it's so hard to control! I can't bear the thought of what faces the people I have known since childhood, I understand, I will control the power I have but I curse Vasconcelos and he will pay for his crimes.'

Aleixo took her hand and pulled her gently towards him, 'Now that I can live with. Come let's go I will have to help at the slave market and I would rather get you Amara and Fugra Away first if I can.'

leaving the wooden prison that had been home for so many months felt like a relief, a weight lifted from Irisa's chest, she breathed in the Salty humid air greedily and for a few moments felt her soul lift into the cotton clouds of the soft blue sky then she readied herself, hardened her heart and faced the tiny port where they were about to land, ready to face the next part of the journey she knew had to be endured, She was however determined that Vasconcelos would not be part of their lives for long and that they would survive.

Aleixo followed behind the Captain, along with Pero. The other slaves herded the men, women and children into the dusty sand and made them sit in silence.

Vaconcelos Made his way to the small boarded area on the beach, set with the chairs for those of importance, several already taken . Vasconcelos stopped at one man dressed impeccably despite the arid heat, mopping his sweaty brown with an equally expensive lace handkerchief.

'Ah! Governor Johnston! What a pleasure to meet with you in the flesh, much better than those impersonal correspondences we have to wait months for!'

Johnston gave a thin smile that didn't reach his eyes.

'Indeed! Call me Robert, Please. I hope you've brought me some strong slaves, we have a bigger crop this year and there is much to do. Did you bring me any good fillies then? I need some for the house, damn wife keeps moaning about lack of slaves.'

'Now Robert, there I can help you, I have a slave for myself who is particularly wholesome! Might help your wife as a maidservant but she may also suit your tastes too from what I've heard!.'

They both laughed heartily, Johnton raised his stick, quickly bringing a slave to them, dressed in a black uniform with a white shirt that smothered his frail physique and made him look like a small boy in his fathers clothes.

'Ah Adam, bring us rum, two glasses, now'

Vasconcelos cocked his head to the side with curiosity, 'Adam?'

Johnston laughed, 'Well of course, he is my first!'

They laughed hard together at their cleverness and wit, until the rum arrived and they hunkered down to do business.

'I do have a rather unique slave for sale this time Johnston, bloody useful sort she is, she's old but her knowledge of medicine is beyond compare, she's kept many of my slaves and men alive on this middle passage. I can do a good deal if you take her along with the house slave. I'm here for your Virginian tobacco but I need victuals for the return journey. We could do a deal for the two if you could help us locate water, rum and food.'

Johnston smiled, 'let's have a look at your goods then man.'

They made their way across to the group of

slaves, Johnston suddenly alert and interested. He made the slaves remove their tunics, poking at their sinewy muscles with his dress stick, making them move this way and that. Within half an hour he'd picked over thirty slaves, mainly strong looking males who could be put to use in the fields. He then started to move through the women, using the same inhumane process to choose them, some for the home and some for the fields. He called his slave handler over and asked him to take them to the plantation and the slave accommodation, before they left to await a news terror, he addressed them:

' I am Governor Johnston. I am now your new owner, your Master. When you address me, you will call me thus. He gave them a lurid smile before continuing. Now I am not a cruel man, you have had a long trip, there will be no work today but be ready for the dawn tomorrow, if you try to escape, you will be brought back, try again and you will be hung. If you abide by my rules, you will find me a fair master, you will be housed and fed in return for your work. Now follow Stowerton, in my place he is your Master, you may call him Sir or Mr. Stowerton.'

He nodded to the slave handler, 'Now take them to their new homes and make them wash, they damn well stink to high heaven.Now Vasconcelos, what about these 'special' slaves then?'

Irisa gripped her tunic, trying to suppress the anger she felt in her heart at the animalistic way they had inspected her people, her friends.

'Mmm, he said, turning Amara on the spot, Now you are a pretty piece are you not? I think you would brighten my house, indeed. Now we need a chambermaid, you like beds, girl? I think you could make them and then we could use them!' He gave a deep laugh that went straight through Amara's heart. She didn't have time to answer, he nodded at Fugra 'So, you are a crone then? Why should you have a privileged position within my household?

Fugra slowly raised her head until she was looking straight into his cold dark eyes. 'I will keep your 'property' alive so they can keep working for you, I'll save you some money, as will this girl' she grabbed Amara and pulled her closer. ' We have knowledge of herbs and medicines that will keep your family well in this dry heat dull of disease, we can birth children yet to come, safely into the world, we have proved this with the shit pigs that took us from our homes as well as our fellow people. It is either enough for you or it is not, however we come together, we work together.'

Fugra did not look away and neither did Johnston, although as Fugra continued her stare he began to sweat and look distinctly uncomfortable.

'Ahh!' he laughed 'A bit of spirit! That's what we need. I think you'll be a god send, we don't have a doctor for over a hundred miles, you'll share a hut together, you will come when called, do you understand?

'Oh yes Master we hear you.' answered Fugra, filling her reply with as much sarcasm as she could although she felt it may be lost on him. 'What a weak willed rat!' she thought.

The Governor looked away, feeling uncomfortable. He could feel a tingling on his back and turned around to see what was the cause. There was no one but the Captain, his man and the man's slave, he must be imagining things, this damn heat must be getting to him.

'Right Vasconcelos, bring your man, the slave, let us move to the plantation house, my 'Bellewater' Mrs. Johnston will be awaiting us with cold beer and warm food. Let's settle our finances shall we? I'll show you the best damn tobacco you have ever seen, smelt or tasted!'

The Governor shouted to his slave, 'Adam, get Joshua to bring the carriage for us, everyone else can walk, quickly now boy!'

With a nod the boy scurried away, only turning his back to the Governor when he was almost out of sight, then ran like the devil to the huge building in the distance.

Vasconcelos, Irisa and Aleixo began to gather their things as the Governor wandered over to them. He pointed to Irisa, 'Obviously she'll have to join the others and walk.' He gave Aleixo a thin smile.

Irisa felt herself tense, Aleixo grabbed her hand, 'she stays with me' Aleixo replied firmly.

Johnston laughed and looked at Vasconcelos.

'Surely he jests Sir! I'll not put a slave in my carriage! I am the Governor!'

Vasconcelos stared at Johnston with an icy glare.

"Well now Governor, you're right it is your carriage, but this is my man, he comes with me, he's rather partial to his slave so if he says she's coming, then that's what's happening. I do not have to sell you these slaves. I have not signed or received coins for them yet! There are many plantations along this coast that would welcome more slaves. Make your choice

Governor.'

'Well, I am sure that this is not appropriate but as you say, you hold the cards today Captain, it is your man after all.'

Johnston moved away and started scouring the horizon for the sight of the carriage, clearly embarrassed by the whole confrontation. Aleixo stood in front of his Captain and bowed his head, 'I thank you Sir, for your intervention, Irisa and I are grateful.'

'Mmmm , replied Vasconcelos, I didn't do it for you, I am sick to death of these rich, self important arseholes who have no fucking knowledge of anything and yet they put themselves above us all!'

He smiled at Aleixo, 'But I am partial to that filly! There's something about her and I'm not sure if it pleases me or unnerves me, but I like her!'

They shared a smile, Vasconcelos joined governor Johnston, offering him a cigar - the offer of a gentlemanly truce. The slaves, weary, most terrified were herded together again and walked back to the plantation. They had been spoken to in a mixture of English and African so heard little of what was to become of them next. It was only as they started to walk away from the Governor that Adam began to speak, using the Alladian they knew.

'Do not be afraid, for those of us that have been taken, this is one of the better places you could be brought. He is what he says, a fair man, he will feed you, you will have a bed to sleep in, but you will work till your bones ache and if you disobey, if you steal, if you try to go above your station, you will be lashed, if you escape they catch you, you will be hung, don't try it, it ain't worth the stress and the work, ain't no one ever escaped from this place. Now let's find your huts and get you some water.

Back on shore the carriage arrived pulled by two of the most beautiful creatures Irisa had ever seen. Johnston could see the wonder in her eyes.

'Why girl, these are horses! Have you never seen them before?'

She gently shook her head.

'Well come then, would you like to touch them? I'll show you how.'

He led her to the animals and guided her hand to their manes. Irisa felt no malice from the man, he seemed genuine in his intentions. This would not be a victim of her God's wrath.

Vasconcelos poked Aleixo in the side.

'See, I told you that woman of yours was special! How did she make that miserable old goat do that then?'

'I know she's special, that's why I picked her.' grinned Aleixo.

They made their way into the carriage, all looking around them, becoming more astonished with every yard that they travelled with just how vast the plantation had become. The horses began to trot away from the shore, when a shouting could be heard, getting louder and louder as it homed in on them. The Governor began to remonstrate ' What is the damn problem now" These damn slaves can be more trouble than they are worth some times! As if they have the audacity to call out to me!'

Vasconcelos leant out of the carriage and turned to the source of the shouting, sighing as he did so. 'Oh damn it, it's Father Francisco! I thought I told him to stay aboard.'

The calls became louder as he approached out of breath and incensed,

'Wait! You there, stop! They can not go to the house without me! I am a man of God! God's own man left to fumble through the grubby foreshore like a wretched seagull! Stop, I say!.'

Governor Johnston gave a light chuckle, 'Ah, yes! I'm sorry Father, in the hustle and bustle I forgot you were on the ship. I hope you have found the voyage bearable, we are ready for your religion here, they're god damn heathens don't you know!'

Father Francisco's breathing began to slow. The carriage had come to a final stop and the priest climbed clumsily aboard, sweating in the searing heat beneath all the layers of religious wear. He struggled to climb into the carriage, in the end Vasconcelos unceremoniously pulled him in so they could re-start their short journey to the house.

'I thought you had planned to stay on the ship until we were finished with the slave's Father? Why are you amongst us now?'

Vasconcelos was ired, irritated, he had no love for the priest or religion, he thought him pompous and that he had a tendency to kindness towards slaves when Vasconcelos had told him time and time again that the best thing for the savages was a firm hand and a good beating if you disobeyed. To bring them to the one true religion, he would have to be harder than that or they'd remain worshipping those ridiculous gods and harbour those women who were witches.

The priest looked down to his hands, wringing them in a nervous habit. 'I had worried about how the slaves would be treated, I can not turn them to the true religion if they are disabused, I needed to see for myself and I am anxious to begin the plans for the church, 'Igreja da Misericordia' 'Our Church of Mercy' it will be a shining beacon in the new world and God will know we have not forsaken him by travelling so far away from all we know.

Johnston guffawed, 'Well now that was a fine sermon preached unto us was it not! I am well aware of how to look after savages that come to these shores, you will find they are christian, good and work until they drop, as of course they should, but, in return they are housed well and fed well ad now they will have access to medical care with the arrival of Vasconcelos's midwives! So kindly do not lecture me when it is my money which gives you the opportunity to have your own church man!

Francisco reddened and held his head high.

'Obviously I meant no offence Sir, I am merely doing my job as emissary to God on Earth, it would be remiss of me if I did not make it my business to know how the congregation are cared for. I apologise for offending you, I am indeed grateful for the funds and labour to build the church and look forward to serving your household as your personal priest. '

'Well countered my man! I mean, Father! Yes

indeed my wife in particular is looking forward to your arrival and I thank you for the hardship you must have endured to reach this heat scorched land to serve us. I just hope you know how hard a task you've been burdened with by your church and your so-called benevolent God.'

The priest nodded his acquiescence and recommenced wringing his hands in earnest. As they began to close in on Bellewater house, Irisa looked in wonder at what her eyes told her but her mind could not believe, a building too large to be real, beautiful white columns holding it up, a round tower atop the roof, windows all the way from ceiling to floor, she marvelled that it could stay up at such a height. She could not picture what lay within but the visage alone took her breath away.'

'Sir, it is magnificent!'

There was no outrage from the Governor now at the fact that a slave had spoken to him, he answered with pride, 'Yes she is dear isn't she? I built this when there was nothing else here but mud and Built it from scratch, my wife of course has commandeered the inside, it is all, thankfully to her taste.! '

The horses followed their trail, leading down a white stone path, into the driveway of the grand building. Awaiting then she could see a group of white folk, dressed similarly to the Governor in richly detailed fabrics that shimmered in the sunlight. The black folks that she could see were dressed in uniforms; cream dresses in a thick cambric, pure white aprons and caps. To her amusement the men wore shirts, waistcoats, breeches and shoes with buckles so shiny they dazzled like stars in the deep night sky.

As the carriage came to the entrance there was a frenzy of activity, the Governor was helped down and fussed about, whilst he spoke privately to his wife.

Irisa had never seen such pale skin before, almost translucent, pure, clear and glowing. How did she keep so pale in this heat?

The Governor turned with a grand hand gesture and gave his oratory;

'Welcome to Bellewater House my friends, this is the delightful Mrs Johnston, my wonderful wife Anna, this is my manservant Joshua,' he gave the small black lad a shove until he spoke.

'Welcome Sirs, I am happy to meet you.'

Johnson sighed loudly, 'I *am* boy! I *am*, not I am.' He gently shook his head. 'Some of these people we can train but they have no manners you know.'

Irisa didn't meet anyone's gaze, she was just in awe that this poor boy had learnt to speak another language so well, she realised that it was not evil but ignorance that slicked off the Governor in waves, ignorance of mankind and of the natural world that he mistakenly felt he could and should control.

'Now Anna, my dear, this is Captain Vasconcelos, who has brought us the most wonderful crop of slaves, this is the right hand man, Aleixo and this is Aleixo, well err, his.'

'Partner' injected Aleixo forcefully, Irisa suppressed a smile.

'Yes, well, quite, my dear Anna, I think you will find her fascinating, maybe she could help you to dress for dinner later?'

'I'd be happy to' Irisa answered gently, she could feel the loneliness and despair emanating from this woman, maybe she could help her.

Aleixo however stood directly in front of the Governor.

'I remind you Sir, she is not my slave, she is my partner, either that is accepted or we stay on the ship with the crew.'

Johnston looked nervously around him, ' Well

yes, she could serve us for dinner if we can find suitable attire for her. But I cannot in all God's graces treat her as an equal. God's beard, she's a bloody woman as well as a slave! You can stay here in the servants quarters or join the others in the huts, you can make that choice.'

Vasconcelos glared at Aleixo, whose face had coloured with anger, 'Sorry old man, he is quite attached to his woman, I'll reprimand him.'

The Governor's wife stepped forward, 'They'll be no need for that Sir, if your companion would like to accompany me, I'd be glad to have another female to talk to, she need not serve me, my husband can be quite proper, he despairs at me at times for my inappropriate social ideals but I don't hold with all these fancy manners, please call me Anna, we will leave the men to talk business.'

She gave her soft, creamy, unblemished hand to Irisa who gave a gentle nod to Aleixo and followed whom she thought as a graceful ghost into the tranquil building. Irisa followed Anna aimlessly, unable to take in the grandeur, the beautiful furniture, what was it all for? Why did they need so much space and so many fine things, dripping with gold?.

Irisa became nervous as they approached the

grand staircase. Anna turned, 'Why, come now, we're going to my rooms, why are you suddenly so nervous? Is it my colour? - she gave a deep sigh- I suppose you have been told that you must behave in a certain way when in the presence of 'my kind' Please don't, I can't abide it.

'Ma'am, I have been told all my life how to behave in front of white folks but in truth it's not you that scares me, it's these! She gestured to the wooden staircase, I've never seen the like before, we live in one room safe on the earth in my home'

'Oh my, well I never thought! Well this is how we get to the next floor, to more rooms, they are solid and safe I assure you.'

With a little more confidence Irisa tentatively travelled up the staircase and followed Anna into a room that she felt was just how it would be in the next life. It was filled with the largest bed she had ever seen, with billowing silk curtains around it, at the windows fluttered thin cotton sheets, thin as the wings of the butterflies in the trees, thin embroidered cottons and heavy drapes, soft and rich in colour. Furniture the colour of burnished gold held bottles and jars of potions and liquids, taller cupboards that she assumed held this woman's beautiful clothes.

‘It’s beautiful Ma’am it truly is.’

‘This is my favourite part of the house, it is ‘my part’ and the only people who come here are my maid and my daughter, thank goodness. Now come, sit with me.’ She indicated two chairs, upholstered in a vibrant floral pattern, enveloped in gold braiding, a dark, shiny wooden table between them. ‘ I am sorry my dear, I know you have been led to believe that all white people think in a certain way and the sad truth is that many do, but not for me. I was raised by working class people, in a large family. I was lucky I had my looks and guile and when I saw the Governor I knew he could be my way out. Not everyone was happy with our union, so we decided to accept the commission and come here to start a new life together on the tobacco plantation. I had a romantic notion of living life on a type of farm I suppose, I had no idea that just as we had been looked down upon we would be repeating this behaviour upon fellow human beings., I abhor it! I put up a front when I have to, but my husband knows how I truly feel. For some reason, when I saw you I sensed that I needed your friendship, oh I’m sorry I am rambling again I can’t explain myself properly.’ she gave a gentle laugh, ‘forgive me, lets have some fresh lemonade.’

Anna called her maid, Irisa watched the interaction closely. The maid came in smiling and relaxed, ‘ Yes Ma’am?’

‘Could we please have some lemonade Lillabelle? How are you today? How’s that boy of yours?’

Lillabelle gave a generous smile in return, ‘Ma’am he is doing good, he on fresh milk now so I aint so tired, thank you Ma’am.’

‘When you leave today make sure the cook gives you some of that fresh creamy milk we have, he’ll like that.’

‘Yes, Ma’am’

Irisa felt the genuine interest and care from Anna and the way Lillabelle responded told her she felt happy and safe here, whether she was working for a white mistress or not. She felt none of the edge she’d experienced with the Governor, he seemed a weak man, with weak vices and Irisa could sense he was not a source of happiness for Anna. The monstrous had pricked up their ears and souls when she had been close to him, he had a sickly heart.

Anna sat back in her chair, ‘So you have a man who cares for you Irisa, hold onto him, he must care deeply for you to fight for you so openly.’

‘He is very good Ma’am, he started by owning me, then I think we just fell into each other's hearts, now we own each other.’ she gave a shy smile.

‘You must call me Anna.’

Irisa leant forwards, ‘Can I ask you a personal question Anna?’

‘Why of course, I rarely get to speak to another female unless it’s the Governor's influence or money they seek, then they are so pro slave that I daren’t open my mouth for fear of speaking from my heart. What would you have me tell you?’

‘Forgive me but you seem to have a good and kind soul, I sense you have had much hardship in your life and little love, yet the Governor sings your praises all the time, I don’t understand him.’

‘Ah well you see he is no diplomat so it is I that has to wine and dine them and make sure he does not come out with anything crass, I suppose he is grateful for the support.’

‘Is there love though?’

‘Oh there was once, when we were young and escaping the gossips and making a new life, we had our darling Rosa and apart from having to accept that his business in the slave trade, we were happy. Then I had a son, Albert, born before his time, he took only a few breaths. I have not been able to abide wifely duties since then and our dear Governor can not understand why any woman could not fall at his feet and demand nights of passion. Love seems to have drifted since then, I can not risk being with a child again, the pain is too much to bear.'

Anna shed small crystal-like tears that slowly dripped down her delicate face.

'Why not just take tea for this?'

'My dear we are English, we drink tea all the time!'

Irisa shook her head, 'No, this is a tea we make at home, it uses a few simple herbs, it stops a child being formed, it means you can have intimate relations without fear of creating offspring, how can you not know this?'

'Oh Irisa, could you show me, could you teach me?'

'I can try, I will show Lillabelle, then she can make it for you, you must make sure that you take it every day.

By the time the group had once again gathered at the grand hall for supper a deal had been done. Vasconcelos was happy to stay for one month to ensure the investment was a sound one and that if the

Governor was happy after that time then Vasconcelos would earn the right to send more slaves the following year and to go away well paid in tobacco for this group. Aleixo had been reluctant, he had been keen for he and Irisa to begin their own lives but he was persuaded that if Irisa could be useful to Anna, then they might at least have one have an ally whilst staying at the wicked plantation.

Chapter 25- Impressions

It was difficult to settle in the house, they had enjoyed the freedom to be together on the Juniper during the long months of the voyage, but as an unmarried couple the Governor could not agree to Aleixo and Irisa sharing a room, even if he tried to put away the fact that she was a slave. In a compromise, Irisa had been allowed to share the maids quarters with Lillabelle, whilst Aleixo was granted a small room close to the Captains. The priest however settled in a grand room that he felt became his station and quickly started his mission of sourcing the best position for the church in this new parish of Virginia.

The grounds were vast, edged with wildwood, filled with trees from the most luminescent lime to the deepest of greens. The light fell between the wildwood making it feel magical. Irisa often explored the wildwood, along with Lillabelle, showing her any herbs she found that they could gather, then showed her how to use them. Irisa revelled in the calm quiet rustling of the trees and the slight breeze that blew through them and gave them both respite from the humidity.

Her first task of showing Lillabelle how to

prepare the herbs to prevent a pregnancy were well received by Anna and with the confidence of not becoming with child, she took the Governor back into her bed, they both glowed with a new found love for one another and it was a much more pleasant atmosphere to be within.

Herself and Aleixo stole time to walk together, sometimes to the beach, on rare occasions when they were sure they were not being watched, they made love in the sand, laying together in their afterglow watching the waves lap onto the shore.

However, Irisa could not ignore that however comfortable they were, the reason they were here was abominable. On her second day she had asked Adam to show her around the plantation. She had stroked the long silky leaves in the tobacco fields and inhaled their thick, pungent scent. As it dried, the harsh acrid smell filled the air as she watched the fields being sweetened - burnt ready to till the land for the next crop. It wasn’t until she was brought to the slaves' homes that she lost her heart and her anger grew again. She could feel the claws of the monstrous begin to hook into her, to swell with indignation as she grew angrier.

Most lived shoved tightly together in small huts

with little more than water, blanket and a bunk. The sanitation was poor and the scent of every imaginable bodily fluid pervaded the air from the open sewers.

The men seemed happy enough, although many were so exhausted that they dropped into a sleep that they could not be awakened from until they felt the gentle sunrise on their skin and knew they had to rise and begin it all again. She witnessed as one man was brought back from the cutting fields, he died of heat exhaustion and was bundled away as though his body was an embarrassment, swiftly a new slave was assigned the dead man's tasks and as quickly as that another human was written off as damaged goods.

Sickened, she made her way to the hut that Amara and Fugra had been given. To be fair the Governor had kept his promise, only two of them shared it, they had a straw pallet mattress, ample blankets for the cold nights, lanterns, food and the supplies they would need to try and treat others on the plantation.

Fugra was more than happy with her situation, although she was fearful for Amara's future, her skills, her youth and beauty being against her chances of survival in such a place.

'We have a lock fitted on this door!' Fugra

shouted triumphantly.

'We grew sick of those love struck, sick men hanging around our hut. I know at least three girls that have raped by fellow slaves in this dingy place. I fear for Amara's safety but now at least they can't get in without us knowing about it.

'Oh Fugra, is it really so bad? What must we do? Do the men not get punished?'

'Fugra chuckled, 'Oh they get their comeuppance, they are flogged until their flesh splits, the damn white slavers checking to see if we are as black on the inside as out. Stupid pigs! Trouble is, it doesn't stop the white men raping the slaves, oh that's ok, that's what we're for apparently.'

'Well then, we need to do something, our people are so misused!'

Fugra sighed and Amara sat up from the bed.

'Irisa what are we to do? Kill them all? Then what? They'd get another plantation owner who comes to take over and start it all again.

Irisa frowned, 'Well the Captain has agreed to stay for a month. It gives me time to find a way to let our people free.'

Amara hugged her knees close to her chest.

'I think we'd be better off focusing on staying

alive first!'

*****

That evening Irisa was quiet as she helped Anna dress for dinner.

'What's wrong child?'

'I've had a tour of the plantation with Adam today. I asked to see it all. I loved the colour and scent from the plants, I loved the air and the heat. Then I was taken to the slave quarter.'

'Ah'

'How do you bear it? You say you don't hold with people being treated that way, how can you bear to watch the violence and the mistreatment of human beings, treated worse than pigs in pens?' tears began to fall down Irisa' cheeks, they cooled her face that was flushed with aggression.

'Well my dear, I don't agree with it but I have learnt to accept that I can not change it, it is what my husband does. I am as much a slave to him as our slaves are to us. For my daughter's sake I have to stay. If I were to leave, I would have nothing, she would not be brought out into society to make a good match, why should she suffer for my choices? So I stay, I don't look too closely, I don't listen too hard, I don't go to the slave quarter. I treat my maids with respect and I choose not to see the seedy side of my husband's career. It is not right but it is a way to survive.'

'Then I'd rather not survive!'

'That's because my dear, I sense you are far stronger than me.'

'Now, enough of this talk, I want you to go to my bed, there is a box on there, can you give it to me.'

Irisa gently lifted the box and passed it to Anna and with that she felt dismissed. Irisa complied despite the irritation that bubbled, how could Anna just push everything aside? Yet in a lot of ways she could identify with her, at least with Aleixo she had been given a chance of a life that she may want to live with him,knowing all before she made that choice. She knew that loving him, being with him was a decision she'd made from a place of honesty, clearly Anna was as trapped as the servants she owned.

Irisa placed the large box on the floor in front of Anna who began to smile and bade Irisa open the package. Irisa opened the box to reveal layers of soft, colourful tissue paper, it felt to her that she was putting her hands through clouds, it was so soft and so light. Eventually the layers opened onto a beautiful dress. It was too plain for Anna but it was beautiful with a fitted, corseted bodice, full skirt of silk, ranging from mid to a rich deep sapphire blue.

'It's beautiful' Irisa whispered

'It's for you.'

'For me?' Irisa frowned, not quite believing what Anna was saying.

'This is a gift from me for all your help. The Governor is a kinder, gentler man since returning to my bed and I have you to thank for that Irisa. You came from the sea, your soul is with the sea, so I hoped this gown would remind you of that and make you remember the ocean and better times.'

'I don't know the words to give you thanks, Anna this is too much'

'Nonsense girl, now put it on for dinner, I would have you attend me tonight.'

Irisa felt the silk slipping over her body, like the water from home; soft, warm,gentle and caressing. Lillabelle helped her force her tight curls into soft ringlets and finally, feeling like a Queen, she bashfully followed Anna into the dinning hall.

Aleixo's mouth was agape as he glimpsed her, Irisa flushed in response. The Governor stepped forward and took her hand,

' Well my dear, now look at you! How can I refuse to let you join us when you look like a treasure captured from the ocean.'

'That was my intent James, now put her down so we may eat.' interjected Anna.

He moved slowly to his wife's side, laughing, 'You are of course as radiant as ever my dear, of course it is your skill that has made Irisa glow.'

Chapter 26- Knowledge

Irisa made sure that she walked around the scorched plantation every day, breathing in the thick clean air, the tangy scent of the plants that grew from the rich earth, the musicality of the trees as their branches rustled in the light breeze, so unfamiliar to her, from rich to poor she took notice of who were the bullies, who were kind hearted, who held malice for another. She also began to understand the value of the crop that was being harvested and stuffed into large crates ready to cross the ocean. Payment for the souls who almost died growing it.

She learnt what made the crops grow, what hindered them and how superstitious the Governor and his family were of the slaves they owned. They forbade the slaves and servants to worship the Gods from their homeland, although late at night between the huts, they still gathered and sang songs of their homeland around a fire, drinking moonshine made from a few stolen potatoes and a hidden still, dancing long into the night after the sun had set behind the Governor's house. The white folk ignored this as much as they could, sensing they would come off worse if they stopped such practice, although they made no attempt to conceal their disgust at how ‘the savages’ worshipped Gods that ‘did not exist.

Once she had gathered all this knowledge in her head, storing it so she could use it to the advantage of her people, she began to plan in her head. The tentative thoughts of how her situation could change. She knew she could not just walk away from it, however she needed to be sure that she found a way to keep her friends and the Governor's wife and daughter safe, because when she unleashed the monstrous from her soul, an evil capable of devouring everything and everyone in the plantation would be let loose to seek revenge.

One evening the umber orange sun melted low into the horizon, she left her room and made her way To Amara and Fugras hut. Her cover was to collect the herbs to prevent a child for her mistress, in truth she wanted to discuss strategy with her friends, she knew that her thoughts were dangerous, that if she could work them, many would die and they would have to leave quickly even if she successfully managed to work her gift.

Fugra and Amara were at a small table grinding leaves. They looked up and smiled in greeting at Irisa’s arrival.

'Ah, are we to call you Lady Irisa now?'

Irisa, full of anxiety about what she was about to discuss, felt irritated at Fugra;s petty jibes. 'Don't be so damn sarcastic Fugra! A finer dress does not make me a finer person as well you know. I want to talk to you both, I need to work out how to release my gift to give us time to get away from here, to free those that wish to leave and to rid this damn place of those that cannot see beyond the colour of a skin.'

'Well best you sit down, I have a little intsenga left, I'll make us a tea, come Amara, join us, I suspect we'll all have a part to play in this.

By the time the sun was falling from the sky and the deep blue night had blackened the earth with its shadow, she came away from Fugra, confused but certain that there would be a time for her to go ahead with this. She prayed that it would be soon, she had no idea that fate held a slightly different course for her.

Chapter 27-Savages?

The morning dawned and Irisa rose early, the sun's early primrose glow filling the air with a diffused light. She was not required to help the Governor's wife that morning, instead she and Aleixo were summoned to the grand drawing room. Irisa was nervous as she walked into the vast echoing space, filled with the couple's riches. Ceramics, glass of the gaudiest colours, statues and silver were abundant everywhere she looked. It seemed to Irisa unnecessary, they had no purpose apart from looking pretty. The Governor and his wife, sat together on a beautiful embroidered couch, edged intricate wooden designs, covered with gold leaf, drinking tea from tiny china cups.

Irisa stood awkwardly, still feeling ungainly in the many layers of cloth she had to wear now the Governor's wife had seen fit to 'give her a splendid wardrobe.' To Irisa it made no sense to wear thick, sticky materials in a heat that felt like a furnace, sh'd rather be in her cool cotton and linen simple dressed with one underskirt, she fidgeted under the gaze of her 'superiors'

'Ah there you are' bellowed the Governor, sweat

dripping down the sides of his manicured face, he fanned himself ineffectively with a limp silk handkerchief. ‘Come, join us, we need to talk about savages!’

Aleixo grabbed Irisa’s hand, he had known she would tense at the word, just didn’t want her to explode, they only had a few weeks before they could return to ship and he wanted to make it with them both alive and free.

‘Savages Sir? Do you mean the slaves we brought with us>’

‘No, no! Not those savages, the ones who live here, the ones we have to make damn deals with! They say it’s their land and we have to pay them for it! Imagine paying slaves for their property, is that not ridiculous! But there we go, that’s what it takes to live in a place such as this.’

The Governor's wife turned her head away, busying herself with the task of pouring the tea. Irisa knew that she abhorred her husband's ideals but was as powerless as the slaves she employed or took for herself to change it.

‘So, Aleixo, we have just started dealing in beaver pelts, damn great beasts they are, eat all the damn wood, block the river, anyway the Indians- the natives who were here when we claimed the land have a great bartering system for them already. We need someone whom they will trust and someone who will be firm, we need to negotiate a trade deal with the buggers'

'Well, I'm honoured you find me trustworthy Sir.'

'Yes well um, sorry Aleixo but it's not you they trust, it's your slave here. The Indians visit our compound at various times during the year, they have heard about your great skill with herbs and medicines, The Sachem's wife is ill, their feathered quacks can't seem to cure her, they've agreed to trade with us if you visit and take Irisa with you, just for a few days, all in good faith of course, you'll be in no danger.'

Aleixo held Irisa's hand, 'she is my partner, not my slave and I will only agree to this if she agrees, I do not force women into compliance Sir.'

Aleixo was furious that he and Irisa were being used in this way, well aware that there was not really an option to turn down what had been suggested.

Irisa spoke gently, ' I will go to see if I can help this woman, it is important to share medicines and knowledge, that's how we survive, however I will go as their equal, not as masters who demand trade and respect, we have not earned that yet and I assume neither have you or your work force if you see them as savages,'

The Governor reddened in the face, 'Oh my dear, you mistake my meaning. I am in awe of their skills with skins and bows, but I have no intention of living in a hide hut with them my dear and for that I will make no apology.'

'Well let us agree to disagree and I will go with my own intention as I'm sure Aleixo will.'

'Aleixo nodded,'It makes sense for peaceful trade to start between yourselves, we can help with the export to England as well, there's money to be made here, however, I am Vasconcelos's man and he will expect a share of any profit we negotiate.'

'Agreed young man, I would not see him out of pocket. Now enough talk of trade, let us share a rum, this damn tea is watery and sickly! I can't wait to get home to have a properly brewed tea.'

In that moment their fate was sealed for no one could know what would happen from the meeting of minds, souls and the will to be free on earth and sea.

Aleixo and Irisa were given the day to prepare, to gather herbs and medicines and anything they thought they could use to encourage the natives to agree to trade with Governor Johnston. Irisa visited Fugra, raiding her medicinal knowledge and dispensary. She reverted back to her original plain dress and covered her hair with a broad white lined bandana, the feeling of returning to her true self with every layer she shed. Then she sought out the priest, she knew he had some knowledge of whom they would meet and hoped this would ensure she approached them with respect for their traditions.

Father Francisco was a whirlwind dithering around the house and was trying to find out when he could start ordering materials for his church, the beacon for Virginia and a place to bring the 'savages' to god. He was rather surprised when Irisa approached him, nervous in his interactions with others Irisa was uncertain as to whether he would be able to manage his priestly duties as well as stand up to the system of order that had begun in the new town and the strength and courage to convince others to come to his religion.

'Yes my dear, what can I assist you with? Have you come to our religion now you are with one of us?'

Irisa fidgeted and tried to ignore her discomfort at 'one of us' but knowing she may need this man, she let it slide. ‘ As I’m sure you’ve heard, Aleixo and I have been told we must visit with the natives of this land and convince them to trade with the Governor as well as heal their leader's wife. I wondered if you could tell me about the tribe? I believe you have met them before?’

‘Yes, yes, I have met with some, they are a crude group, they wear skins you know, animal skins! They have some strange rituals and they commune with different Gods than us, of course there can only be our true Lord but I’m sure they’ll understand. They have traded well with us before, with food and crops but not with the beaver pelts, make wonderful hats don’t you know!’

‘I was thinking more about how to approach without causing offence, I too worship other Gods and will not be converted to a God I do not believe in, so don’t bother with your religious tirades with me Father, I respect your decision to worship whom you do, I hear many from your lands do, but I will never, I am Alladian and I can understand how these people feel with you coming to their homes and telling them that years of tradition are wrong and that they are a lower species than those with white skin!’

‘Oh I meant no offence young woman, I can tell

you that rather like yourself they use plants and herbs as medicines and many are very effective, if they have tried to use them on the chief's wife then you will struggle to save her with yours. Would you like me to accompany you, so I can guide and keep your soul safe? They do have a medicine woman, they call her Mediwin, you should speak to her when you reach their compound, do not be shocked by how they live and show respect to the Chief and you should return safely, again I ask if you would like my help? It would be a good way for me to introduce myself to the tribe.'

'I care not whether you come or not, but we have been asked to go for a specific reason and I will not have you interfere with that.'

'Indeed, well then I will follow you and Aleixo.'

The only other information he could give her were the names of the chief and chieftess, which she could neither pronounce nor remember, he seemed to have a good heart and intention but she would stop him from upsetting those she wished to commune with.

Within the shade of the colonnades and crisp white plaster, she looked up to Aleixo, shielding her eyes from the sun that was already warming the ground at their feet and would soon burn their skin.

He held her hand gently in his.

'Are you sure that you want to go through with this Irisa? I have no idea how they'll react to us, or the useless bloody priest we now have to babysit, I don't know if they'll be offended, curious or ready to fight, I only know that since our people have landed here, we have raped and pilaged their land and their sacred spaces and now we are telling them they must trade with us or loose even more of their sacred earth.'

She removed her hand and adjusted the pack she'd put together, everything she needed tied together in a large sheet, tied around her shoulder and back.

'I have a sense that this journey will be good for us, after speaking with Father Francisco, although he seems to need saving from them himself. I see them as I see my own people, worshipping the Gods and mother nature, respecting one another with a society based not on hierarchy, rather as a collective group, working together for a better future for their children. I welcome their questioning and their resistance. They should be wary of anything that comes from the cruel white folk that have taken everything from them and brought them nothing but death and disease.'

They had only walked a few steps when they

heard angry discourse echoing from the house, Father Francisco stomped heavily into the garden, waving his hand in protest as Governor Johnston emerged slightly breathless having apparently chased after the priest.

'I will not Sir, I repeat I will not torture those poor starved peoples! You are a devil Sir! A devil!'

'How dare you, you ignorant pig! You are not so dense in the head to believe that these people would willingly come to your church because you simply ask it. They are savages! They need to be told what to do and how to do it. Would you rather we all became brown skinned, smoke blowing fools? They chant to Gods that do not exist and you say you will not physically force them to our God! You Sir are the devil!'

Father Francisco was now puce with rage, stuttering as he tried to vent his anger, incensed and disbelieving that this man had proved to be such a trickster. 'I was promised a beautiful stone church to honour Our Lady of Mercy, I have a stinking hut and a room full of wooden crosses that no black man will take! The ones whom you claim to be converted are paying you lip service, they do not believe in our Lord God. Your answer to this is to beat them into submission, starve their women and children to make them agree. How could God condone these acts?'

'If the problem is your guilt at getting your hands dirty, I can provide a well trained man servant, he will beat whomever you tell him to, then your conscience will be clear and we will not need to fear them.'

'You are a fool! If I command another man to complete those acts on my behalf, I would be as guilty in the eyes of God! I have sworn I will not be a part of it, I shall not. After I have accompanied Aleixo and Irisa on their mission, I shall return to England with the Captain and you can rot in this sweltering hole!

The Governor stamped his feet indignantly,'You are denying your betters and not following your doctrine! What about all of us, The American and English, in need of spiritual guidance? Are we not important in your eyes or Gods? I will contact your priesthood and this will not be the end of the matter.'

As the Governor walked back towards the house, he caught sight of Aleixo and Irisa trundling along the driveway with their bundles of belongings, waiting for the priest to catch them up.

'That man is evil, it would be best if we all stopped doing his bidding! I will leave the decision to you but I would advise leaving the idiot here until you return, he can do no good now.'

Irisa, who had admired Father Francisco's speech, found a new liking for him in her heart and was surprised at his courage and fortitude and his will to not go ahead and cause physical pain to an already downtrodden group of people, spoke up, 'I think we will manage with him, won't we Father?' She looked across the gravel as he arrived with a leather bag, tied around him. He smiled in return, 'Yes my dear I believe we will all get along and when I reach these 'savages' I hope they are less savage than you Sir!'
He turned and continued to walk ahead of the pair, who trotted up to him as they left together.

The Governor still had enough bluster to shout out to them,' Make sure you do as you're commanded Sir! I have had my share of insubordination today! My stomach is sick with it!.'

Aleixo smiled slyly and pulled an even larger pack of his own onto his back, ' I feel it providence that has sent us away at this moment, there is only so much dissent the Governor will accept before he implodes and acts, I'd rather we were not here to see it when it does happen. As for the Algonquins that we are seeking, I should have known you would see past the obvious dear one, I feel they will be as enamoured with you as I am. Let's go to the slave quarter, our guide is waiting for us there, we will never find it otherwise. He will take us to the edge of their lands in the East towards the sea, they will have one of their own people there to meet us and to guide us to their homestead. They move throughout the year, they are not easy to find. You sure you're ready for this Father?' The priest nodded and together they made their way into the unknown.

Part 5:

1633-
The Algonquins

Chapter 28 - Native Lands.

It was many hours later when they reached the edge of the natives' land. They were hot, sweaty and eager to take their rest. They had travelled through the flat , sandy loam, rich, tall grassland that swayed in the breeze, resembling rippling water moving in the softest of waves. They travelled further East until they began to meet the forested areas of the Land of Virginia. Irisa noticed that the land was starting to grow steeper and craggier and by the time they were looking ahead for their next guide, they were seeing the foothills of mountains close at hand.

Irisa sat, exhausted and irritated, 'There is no one here! Is this a game to them tol make us travel for the best part of a day when there is no point to it!By the Gods!'

The priest was breathing heavily, squatting on the ground, trying to get his breath back.' I don't think I have ever walked that far in my life! Why could we not have brought some of the Governor's horses.

Aleixo laughed,'Because he doesn't care about us, only that we reach here and get his trade deal done! Besides his horses are not cut out for this land, the foothills have too many crags for a horse used only to travel driveways, to answer you Irisa, from what I hear they are a wiley tribe, they will see us before we see them'

'Indeed!'

Irisa shot up, Aleixo had protectively placed himself in front of Irisa, Francisco was trying to hide behind a boulder, unsuccessfully.There was a deep chuckle as a shape slowly emerged from the near-by trees, dressed in leather skins and feathers, with hide wound and tied around his legs, he held a long wooden bow in his hands.

'I apologise for the fright, I am Wyono, I am Chief Abooksiquin's son. I speak some of your language.'

Irisa sighed with relief, Francisco slowly uncurled his body and eyed the stranger with distrust with an element of awe. She sat up, relieved that these people were clearly not 'the savages' they were portrayed as back at the plantation.

'I am Irisa, from Allada, a land so far away I am unsure if it still exists, this is Aleixo, he comes to do trade talks with your leaders, this is Father Francisco, he comes to help so none of our Gods become angered, We are to see your father?'

The priest opened his mouth to object, Aleixo nudged

him hard in the ribs and whispered, 'Shh man, she is trying to make sure they accept you as well, do you want that arrow stuck in your heart?'

Francisco held back and looked to the Indian.

'I take you, come , follow. I will be slow for you people.' He gave a rich , deep throated laugh and started to walk away at pace.

Aleixo barred Iris from walking as she began to follow the strange man, Francisco stopped suddenly, almost bumping into them.

'Why do you have weapons? I did not bring a gun, I thought we were to meet in good faith, I will not see my woman in danger.'

Wyono laughed again, 'You white people are mad! I bring it so I can hunt food, you should have brought a gun to protect your woman from bears. Tonight we celebrate your visit with a feast, I also come in good faith.'

Aleixo lowered his head, aware he had already managed to offend the Chief's son in the first few moments of their meeting.

'I am sorry, it's just we have been attacked by so many, been used in so many ways, we are wary of new people, I meant no offence.'

The tall man looked down to Aleixo, 'Well this I

understand, follow me, we go to Father now, we need a woman to help my mother , Aleshanee. '

The unlikely group slowly moved through the rocks and trees with varying degrees of agility. It seemed to Irisa that Wyono could fly as he aptly leapt over roots, outcrops, skimming across the landscape, whilst she, Alexio and the priest managed to find and trip on almost every tree root, bulging rock or patch of loose soil. They moved through a dense area of forest on top of a rocky outcrop, where only the most tenacious plants would thrive, coming out into a bright sun filled clearing. Irisa, Alexio and the priest marvelled at the sights before them; in the centre was a large tent formed from wood and hide, surrounding this there were a variety of tents, the same construction but of various sizes, bundles of logs outside some, woman grinding corn outside others, children running freely between the structures, playing, giggling and happy. Above all there was a sense of calm and happiness which pervaded the air.

Wyono turned to them explaining that he was going to fetch his father who would officially welcome them and give them permission to be in their home and then discuss how Irisa could help Aleshanee. He returned with a man looking surprisingly like Wyono but with a hard life written across his face that had aged his skin. He wore leathers on his body and a headdress of the brightest feathers in his hair.

He nodded to Aleixo and Irisa then spoke to them in his native language. Wyono translated; ' My Father welcomes you to the Algonquin, he says you be looked after, give food, shelter, he hopes you help mother, she is precious here, she helps with healing others.

Irisa smiles at the looming Chief,' Chief Abooksiquinn, I will do my best to help your wife and if it is in the power of the herbs and my healing, I will make her well.'

There was a pause as Wyono tried to translate and Abooksiquinn gestured for them to make their way to the large central tent.

Chapter 29 - Secrets shared.

Irisa's breath was taken away as she entered the tent, it was warm and welcoming, there was a central fire, blankets and throws but above all, it brought back memories of Allada. Her deep brown eyes glistened with tears. Wyono noticed and pointed to his eyes and then her face, 'You sad?'

'No, not sad, your home reminds me of mine, the one the white man took me from. I miss my home that is all. Take me to your mother, let's see what we face, this man is to come with me.' she pointed to the priest.

'He may come but he must not mention his God in this place.' he gave Francisco a stern stare, Francisco responded by nodding sagely,

Aleixo was guided to sit with the Chief whilst Irisa made her way to the back of the tent. On a bed of furs lay a middle aged woman, her skin glistening with sweat, making it appear almost iridescent.Long, dark hair lay shining against the light furs, she wore a full length dress that seemed to be made from the tiniest deer hide, decorated with seeds and shells, around her neck she wore an arrowhead on a twine.

Francisco could not help but lean over and stare at this strange creature, whispering under his breath 'she's beautiful'

Irisa stared at him, 'What did you expect? A ranting monster? Please don't believe all others tell you Father, look around you, believe what you see but also what you feel.'

He took a step back as Irisa began to inspect the woman.

Irisa was struck by this woman's aura, sensing her soul more than she visualised her beauty. Gently she held Aleshanee's hand, listening to the beat of her blood as it pulsed through her body. It was slow and weakening, she felt the gentle squeeze of a hand in return, a smile curled on her lips, she was still in this world, Irisa started to feel another pulse, not from the blood but from the woman, sensing her, finding her. She felt herself gasp as she touched the monstrous that lay within Irisa, her God gift. Irisa shivered and removed her hand. Alenshanee gently shook her head and reached out her hand meekly for Irisa, 'Wan - ik, wanik, waniky, waniky!'

Abooksiquinn came to his wife and wiped her brow, he called his son to him and spoke urgently in his ear, Wyono moved closer to Irisa, 'My Father , he say Mother calls you Saviour, she say you have special gift, she say you help us all, you will be our saviour.'

Irisa felt her skin blush with embarrassment. 'I am no saviour, I do have a gift, I can't deny it knowing that she can feel it, it is from my Gods, just as I think your mother has been given a gift from hers. I will try and help your mother, I think we have a connection, that we are similar.'

Aleixo and Fransisco stood abruptly, Aleixo whispered sharply in her ear, ' Are you sure you want to share those types of secrets with a people we barely know, Irisa, please think, this is not just about your safety but the safety of those back at the plantation. The Governor still burns witches you know.'

Francisco gave the sign for the holy trinity and looked pale with fear, although he had the sense to hold his tongue.

Iris smiled at Aleixo,'Oh you have picked a difficult time to distrust me. I felt at home here as soon as we entered their camp, I felt the Chieftess's gift and she felt mine, there would be no point in denying it. I do not feel any threat from these people, certainly not like the threats I feel from your finely dressed associates that just pretend to be polite and courteous when they really despise having a dark skinned woman in their presence.'

Aleixo turned and sat down with a deep set frown on his downturned face, he had not been challenged so directly by her before, he was angry that she could not see he was simply protecting her.

The Chief had been wildly gesturing to his son, who was talking quickly and pointing to Irisa, Aleixo, Francisco and then around the room. There was a moment of sudden understanding of what was happening dawned on his face. He gave a loud 'ah' in recognition then started talking to his son again and gestured for him to repeat what he had said to the group.

'My father, he say, here we no punish people for having gifts that Gods give them, we welcome them, we cherish them, respect those gifts, we know that there is more than this realm, we know there are others, we talk to our dead, we talk to our Gods and they talk back to us, guide us, aid us. He says do not be ashamed of your wife Aleixo, there is no judgement here and no threat from our people.'

Francisco shook his head, 'Am I to believe this? That there is more to this world? That we can all worship different Gods and some receive gifts. If I witness this I believe I will have witnessed a miracle and I will continue on a peaceful mission to serve my own God.

Aleixo bowed to the Chief and returned to the furs on the floor. They were offered small beer, which was gladly accepted. 'I am sorry Irisa, I was scared for you, I am glad you feel welcome here, let's see if you can help the chieftess.'

'I will Aleixo and I believe I can'

Francisco reached out a hand to Irisa, 'May I pray for you while you try and heal her? Maybe we could use all the Gods we have at hand?' He smiled and she agreed.

Irisa stared at Aleshanee, fading away into her eyes. As she picked up her hand she felt a buzzing that moved through her body, she felt a bridge form between her mind and Alanshanee's. She saw Aleshanee through a soft grey mist, moving pictures in her mind. Aleshanee was gathering herbs, moving through the tall swaying grasses. Spring had settled on the land and the animals were awakening and breeding. She saw her reach for a blue cohosh root and stiffen as she saw the head of a large snake, mottled and hidden in the grass, a female, agitated and ready to attack. Less than a second passed and the snake attacked, its fangs biting deep into Aleshanee's velvety flesh, then it withdrew, its job

done. Irisa watched as Aleshanee made her way back through the grass, over the savanna, through the forest to the camp, swaying as she moved now, as her blood cells were being killed by the venom, working its way through her body. Aleshanee had a weak heart and when the poison reached this, it would be the end of this life for her. By the time she reached home, she collapsed and was unable to share what had happened, Irisa heard the word- 'Chu'a'- a snake.'
She sat up and spoke to Wiyono ' she had been bitten by a snake, you say chu 'a' ? It had a copper coloured head, do you know what this is? We have many snakes at our home in Africa but I have not seen one this colour.'

Wyono wiped his face, fear showing in his eyes. 'Oh to God! It is a copperhead snake, she will die! We will lose her, we will' he could continue more as he dissolved into sobs, reaching for his father repeating the word 'chu 'a'' over and over again. His father shaking his head and holding his son tight, muttering to the Gods for release from this nightmare.
Irisa took some Insenga from her bag, asked for stones and ground the leaf to a thick paste which she spread into Aleshanees mouth, she knew as it dissolved into her body, the chemicals would release

and break down, causing her to relax and er heart rate would slow, this might slow the approach of the venom, she knew she had few options, she knew this could be the thing that saved the people she represented or the thing that drove them to war and she was nervous.

'Wyono would you explain to your father I think I can help, that I can remove the venom by calling on the God gift that lets me use the monstrous for our protection, it will be difficult for them to stop once they have removed the venom if I lose control. I can't promise it will bring this Chieftess back, but if I don't try, she will be dead within the hour.'

Wyono translated Irisa's nervous speech. The Chief nodded, the lines deep in his face as he thought carefully about what was being said. He did not reply to Wiyono, he came to Irisa, held her hand and said 'trust' he nodded then began to walk outside the hut, gesturing for all the others to leave.

Aleixo was anxious to stay, to protect Irisa, worried what would happen to her if she failed. Irisa could sense him and his indecisiveness and approached him with empathy. ' It's o.k Aleixo, I love you and I am grateful for your worry but I need to do this alone. The monstrous are dangerous, I will need all my focus to make them stop, you would be a distraction my love.'

He kissed her lips as gentle as butterfly wings, thrumming on leaves. 'I'll be outside, call whatever the outcome, I will be with you my love.' He trundled out of the hut, anxiety ripping through his heart. Father Francisco looked up sheepishly to Irisa, 'I am ready my dear, I will bear witness to whatever happens here.'

Irisa lent over Aleshanee, she held her hand and put it against her heart and her head. Aleshanee gave a nod of acceptance and full of trepidation Irisa began. She let her mind drift, watched as colours melded together, streaks of colour and energy around the tent, she felt her mind growing stronger, her thoughts focussing, she began to feel she was moving more into the other realm than this. Her body began to sway as she began to hum, chanting to the Gods within her, she concentrated on the thick black sound, the darkness that approached her through a mist of golden light. She felt the monstrous tentatively feel out to touch her heart, soul and head, she felt rather than hear Aleshanee gasp as they began to stream into her mind, connected as it was to hers.

The fingers of darkness entwined and encompassed her, and she let it, let it until she could feel the pressure of the malevolence. 'Help me,' she said 'in this realm there is death, it is venom, it is a harbinger of doom, feed upon it, feast upon it, take it into yourselves as you will but you must not touch the soul or the life force of this woman here, she has her own God gift, the gods would be angry,now take it! Take it away from her beating blood and leave her as she was before!.

Irisa's voice crescendoed until she was screaming, 'Take it! Take the death serum, hold it tight into your darkness, let it grow your revenge, darkness and rage! Then leave I command you, leave this pure soul be!'

Irisa felt a sharp pain on her head as the monstrous began to feed on the venom, to suck at it deeply, bringing it into their icy presence. Gradually there was less and less that she could feel from them, she heard Alanshanee murmuring:' Gitchie manitou! Kitchie Manitou,' then she passed out. Irisa screamed as the last of the venom was embroiled into the monstrous, she fought harder and harder to remove them from her mind, she gave one final push to bring all the force she could and knew no more for the next hour.

Chapter 30- Relief.

Irisa began to feel a pulse in her blood, she could feel and hear distant drums, shouts and cries, alarmed, she sat up and tried to make sense of the world around her. As she was released from the cloudy haze of unconsciousness she could make out a singing, drumming, feeling the beat in her blood as it pulsed her back to the light. It sounded joyous and that confused her, why would they be joyous whilst their Aleshanee was lost to consciousness. She attempted sitting up again, this time with more ease and presence, she rubbed her eyes, trying to remember where she was and to reacquaint herself with sights that had been new to her before she was lost to the dark, catching glimpses of the odd familiar item, colour or texture that she remembered, that had stuck in the front of her mind before she tried to heal the chieftess. She looked down and saw that she had been placed on a bed of thick, warm furs and skins, next to the Chieftess who was also rousing, mumbling to herself and reaching out for someone or something.

Irisa moved slowly off the skins and offered the Chieftess the fresh water that had been placed next to them both in small bone cups. She gently tipped the cup to the lips as the realisation that she had healed the woman ran through her thoughts, She she had managed to contain and restrain the monstrous to a particular purpose and for this she was grateful to the Gods.

The priest was sitting cross legged on the floor beside the Queen. He stared at Irisa for the longest time, seemingly at a loss for words. Finally he stuttered, ‘I, I, did I really just see what you did,? did I really just witness a gift from another god? save another with other beliefs? You are a miracle my dear! I will never again question you or your beliefs, I think this world is large enough for us all to pray to those who bring us strength. I am beginning to think I should be praying to you.’

Irisa looked up at Father Francisco, ‘I am grateful for your faith in me, but I have no wish to anger anyone else Father, let’s just be glad it worked and take comfort in the fact that whether it is one good or all of our gods, there is something else in our universe that we can pray to, can gain hope from, that’s enough for me. I am certainly no idol to pray to! ‘ she gave a grunt of laughter and the priest smiled in return.

‘I Understand,’ he rescinded, ‘but I will always be in awe of you, your gods and your power. I do believe I will head off and sleep for a while now, to pray and clear my thoughts. I feel too exhausted to watch any other miracles today.' With that he wandered out of the Chief and Chieftessess hut and Irisa gave thanks that she had another aly she could now rely on to fight her corner if needed.

Aleixo came running into the hut with Wyono, 'You are saved!' Wyono was beside himself, he cried, held his mother gently in his arms stroking her hair and she responded from her drowsy gaze and reached out to embrace her son, comforting him.

'I am saved Wyono, thanks to this woman, she has more of us in her blood than of the white pigs! She has a gift from her gods and we should celebrate!'

Wyono laughed, 'Mother, can't you hear, we are already celebrating! Father ordered it as soon as he knew you would live, come they dance in honour of you.'

Aleshanee removed one of the glossy black feathers that lay in her headdress, that singled her out as Chieftess and passed it to Irisa. 'You put yourself in danger for me, you owe me nothing yet you still tried to save me, this feather is from our sacred bird, it represents strength and loyalty, it is yours now, wear this gift with pride and know you will always have a place here.'

Irisa gently took the feather and tucked it against her own tight black curls, she smiled at the Chieftess. ' It is me who should thank you, this is the closest to home I have felt since I was taken from my own. The joy you take from the world around you, taking only what you need and being content with that, the respect and love for one another in your tribe is a good way to live I think.'

Aleixo put his hand out to steady Irisa as they moved outside the hut. The fire in the middle of the ground was burning bright orange and flickering in the fading light. Dancers leapt high into the air over the flames, men dressed as warriors cavorting around the fire. The elders of the group were beating drums or sticks, the women singing and joining the men in a frenzied dance to celebrate the living Queen and to thank the Gods for her return to life.

Irisa smiled with glee, 'Look Aleixo, look how they celebrate! The clothes, the words may be different but this is so like my home, like Allada, it hurts to remember.'

The air began to fill with a cold breeze, sending shivers through Irisa. Wyono returned with furs for them so they could continue to watch the celebration ceremony until their heads dropped with exhaustion and Aleixo led them to a smaller hut further away from the fire, where enveloped in soft furs they had the deepest sleep either of them had enjoyed since leaving their homes.

Chapter 31 - Nature's Call.

The bright cool morning dawned and Aleixo woke with the certainty that today would be an uncomfortable one after all the joy of those before. Until now he had been here to support Irisa and her skills but now he would have to talk with Chief on behalf of the Englishmen he knew they despised, that held the Algonquins to ransome, that brought in diseases that none of the natives were immune to, wiping out families as swiftly as a killer cat. He was anxious that the fragile trust that had been built up between them in this short space of time would crumble in light of the negotiations around beaver pelts.

Irisa left the hut early, eager to visit with Aleshanee and ensure that the tribe had all the herbs and tisanes to treat her when she left, so she could make a full recovery. She arrived at a hut full of bustle around Aleshanee as she prepared for the day. The women were readying for a fishing trip to the river within the marshes and were collecting baskets to take with them in their shallow canoes.

Irisa was invited as a good luck token, and

laughing agreed to join them, honoured they'd even consider letting her into their small community. She sat perched at the front of a slim wooden canoe, carved from one whole strong tree trunk, carefully picked from their own forests, always after a storm there was much firewood and wood for making anything they needed. Irisa gently trailed her fingers in the cool water of the Rappahannock river as the rising sun warmed her neck and her soul. The silence was complete apart from the quiet chatter of the women as they prepared their baskets. Irisa inhaled the salty air from the brackish water, the baskets were set with ropes, she helped the women as they pulled them back in, gathering the small silver fish, their delicate scales gleaming in the sunshine. They took only what was needed for their families, dropping the youngest fish back into the salty water, giving mother nature a chance to gestate the next haul of adult fish. By the time the canoe was back on shore, Irisa felt calm, sated and happy with the couple of hours of pure work she had taken part in. She excused herself to gather herbs from the marshes that she knew would be effective against the fevers and returned to the Chieftess to administer a soothing tisane.

Whilst the women chatted, Aleixo was trying to

persuade the Chief that agreeing to trade some of their furs with the whites would mean that they would be left alone, that they could then continue to gather whatever furs they wanted once they had met the quota for the Governor. The Chief could not understand why he should take this action. The tribe had for generations trapped enough furs for clothes, blankets, shoes for the winter but they knew that what they took would be paid for in sacrifice of another, why take more than was needed? Why could these white folk at the tobacco plantation not trap their own?

Aleixo thought that discussing British commerce and trade would seem rather nonsensical to a man whose community still held the beliefs of their ancient ancestors, so tried another tactic.

' I have to be honest with you Chief Abooksiquin, the white people on that plantation are lazy, they sit in their building with more than they could ever need but still they want more. They use blacks to work for them until they drop with exhaustion or death, they do not unite together like your tribes, or my community back home. The whites want Ahmik so they can trade with merchants across the sea in their own land of England. The Ahmik pelts are sold for much coin to make fancy hats with little purpose for even richer white folk. They want the coin but they do not want to work.

Abooksiquin frowned. ‘ Then why should we work for the people who stole our land, killed our families with disease or swords,How does this help my people?’

Aleixo paused and sighed, ‘You can trade with them for coins that you can use with other traders who come here, or you could exchange for goods. If the white folk on the plantation are content then they will leave you alone. I fear if they do not get what they want they will try and seize more of your land and send their slaves to do the work and then still take the coin.’

‘Give me time to consider, I will commune with the spirits, with my Wapeka and I will give you my decision tonight. Now Wyono will show you around our camp. I believe you will be surprised how resourceful us ‘savages’ can be.’

Wyono led Aleixo out from the hut into the bright sunshine, ‘Come, I will show you a practice place for young ones, it’s where they learn to hunt, they make laugh when they miss!’ Aleixo followed behind, smiling to himself as Wyono sprinted off across the verdant grasslands, past the women weaving, preparing the corn, and sitting around a group of fat happy, gurgling babies.

Irisa returned from the Marsh, her woven basket brimming with plants, herbs and bulbs she could use for medicines for the tribe and to take back to the plantation and share with Fugra. She took herself to a group of women who sat working together. She sat herself slightly away from the group, not wanting to interrupt them. She began to bundle the stems together with a small piece of corn leaf. She was so engrossed in her activity that she didn't notice two young Indian women slink closer to her. They sat watching intently as she selected the stems, methodically working her way through them. It wasn't until she had run out of corn leaf that she finally looked up, ready to search for some more grass for binding, she almost jumped out of her skin as she suddenly noticed the two women. The women glanced at one another and giggled. They pointed at the basket of plants, then frowned at her. Irisa relaxed, realising that they didn't understand what she was doing. She mimed vomiting, then putting a herb into her mouth, then looking well. They nodded and pointed to a small hut hanging with feathers, shells and bones- their wisewoman she realised. She nodded again and pointed to herself and then the hut, The smile they gave in return reassured her she had gotten it right. The women started to walk towards the hut and indicated for Irisa to follow them, which she readily did, filled with her own curiosity as to what she would find when she got there, would this be another Fugra? Did they use similar medicines and plants for the benefit of the tribe? She had so many fleeting thoughts go through her head that she felt slightly dizzy when she reached the hut.

An elderly woman dressed in feathers and skins, necklaces of shells, feathers and beads hanging over her sagging body. She began speaking quickly without pause. Irisa had yet to pick up any Indian that had stayed with her and began to turn, believing she had been refused entrance by the wisewoman. She was startled to hear a husky 'come woman' in halting English.

She pivoted on her heels and observed the Crone smiling at her. ' Yes I hear your words young one, many whites trade with us here, come, show me your skills.'

Irisa's eyes could not stop looking around the hut, it was filled with a myriad of pots, potions, bones, feathers, dead animals and dried plants hanging from the ceiling, only some of which she recognised. Thick furs covered the floor, a type of mattress in one corner, again covered with furs and rough cloth blankets she believed must be where the woman slept, there was a small table next to the bed and everywhere there were burgeoning dishes of dried flowers, crushed into pastes and powders.

'Sit girl' she croaked, 'I am too old for standing. I hear that you have more gifts than just herbs and medicines. Abooksiquins squaw speaks well of you, she says she has felt your gift as you have felt hers when you healed her, she said it made her feel scared too, your gift, as if it could easily be an evil thing.'

Irisa replied sheepishly, 'I didn't think that she was going to share that, do people here talk about their God gifts? I did, at home but only with my family and friends. If I were to talk about it in front of white people, they would burn me! They would think I'm a witch.'

'They have no sense girl! That's why they starve, fight, kill, for one man having one more pig than another, more land, more everything! Stupid pale men have never learnt how to live together as we know, as you know.'

Irisa nodded sagely, 'They are too afraid to believe in what they cannot see, they deny themselves much and are greedy instead for land and riches, although I do believe that is not every white, but certainly those who already have everything, those are the ones who can't stop wanting and fighting to get more.'

'Mmm,' mumbled the Crone 'and everyone else's lands too.' she shook her headband stared intently at Irisa, until feeling uncomfortable, Irisa looked away.

'She my daughter,' Irisa startled and looked up questioningly, 'Abooksiquins Queen, she is my daughter, is why I have so much standing here. I am a powerful threat if he mistreats her.' she cackled to herself and looked back towards Irisa, ' He is a good man, good Chief, he cares for the land, animals, sea, wish there were more men like him in the world, not those white men who come take everything.'

Irisa stared at her, ' Not all white men and women are bad, some of them have also been hurt and had the world taken from under them. I met a man whose world was broken when dark folks took his people and land, then to save his family he did the same. He knows that is wrong, he wishes to help his family and start a simpler life with me. ' Irisa sighed deeply. 'In my home, we live as you do, working together, living together as one family, caring for our earth. I miss my home here more than when I am stuck in that big mansion with the Governor's wife. She feels as trapped in her world as we do in ours, it is a curse to be a woman and have intelligence.'

The Crone nodded, 'That it is, girl! But there are some places where it is not as bad. I think you need to think carefully about what you said, it seems you love the man but not his world. You have big decisions you will need to make and they will not all be able to be made with your heart alone my dear. Now, come, show me your basket and what your gatherings are for. I hope we can share some ideas about medicine at least.'

They very quickly became engrossed in what each plant and herb was used for and began to discover that much of their medicine was the same if not similar although there were things they could add to make new or more potent medicines with both their knowledge working together, true wise women. Irisa felt content discussing poultices, how to blend them, make tisanes for the weak and weary and she found that time passed easily in the old Crone's company.

Eventually they paused, Irisa asked for hot water and brewed them a nettle tea,fresh with mint, which they both greedily consumed, relishing its pure natural scent. Irisa prepared to leave but the old woman placed her wrinkled hand upon Irisa's and quietly said, 'Please do not go, show me your God gift and how it works. I think I could help you focus this gift if you would let me, focus it so you can use it to get away from the white men.'

Irisa gently shook her head, ' I'm not sure that's a good idea, it can become frightening. There needs to be preparation and control and a clear point in using it, otherwise it is dangerous and it could end many lives.'

The Crone gave a sharp nod. ' Good, I hoped this would be true, we may need to end lives to be safe, now tell me first what it looks like, what we call it, how we stop it, then I will tell you my thoughts.'

With some trepidation but sensing the reality in the Crone's words, Irisa agreed. They made themselves comfortable in the furs and Irisa explained how she had used her gift against her violent father and the abusive village man. The mediwinn- Chenoa, who was named after the beautiful white doves that filled the trees with their soft cooing as the dawn light filtered through the dark forest - listened intently as Irisa explained how she called the monstrous from the dark place her Gods had given her access to, how she found them resting uneasily in the darkness.

She finished her tale and looked nervously to Chenoa, not realising how nervous she had been until she felt herself relax in the warmth of Chenoa's old, wise eyes and smile.

'You have Kitchie Manitou in you, you have a gift from him that would be dangerous in another's control, but you have a pure soul and it is still pure, you did only what you had to do, what others would wish to do if they knew it was possible, there are many times in your life where you could have used it to your advantage, bt you did not. For this I admire you. Kitchie Manitou has blessed you and I respect that.'

Irisa smiled back, 'In Allada, my homeland, we have many gods, but I think Mami Wata is close to your Gitchie Manitou. Mami is female, she helps heal the earth and the spiritual world, we also have gods of air, fire and earth, everything in balance, this is how you worship too?'

Chenoa gave a smile, 'We do indeed, we are

more similar than I first imagined. How do your people live? Do they have homes like the whites where you've come from?'

Irisa laughed. ' No we do not! We would think it a waste of space and land on which to grow more crops and herbs for ourselves. We have simple but comfortable homes, similar to yours, they are made of wood and we stay in them allo year through. The weather does not change so much in the seasons as it does here. In Allada the early morning sun shone through our spiny jambackto trees and filled the earth with pure light. Like you we were near a river and close to the sea. I feel my spirit drawn to the ocean, feel it try to drag me down and swallow me softly in her gentle clinging waters and caress my skin and soul forever.'

Irisa stopped, suddenly too full of emotion to continue, Chenoa held Irisa's small hand in her own. 'We too believe souls have a place, either in air, fire or water and we give thanks for that.' She patted her hand and replaced it on the furs.

'Chenoa this has been a most precious moment, there have sadly been few since being ripped from my homeland. I have no wish for fine gowns, large houses and money in coins. I am happy by the sea, living with what the earth provides and what the gods will give me to have. I have no idea what my future holds. I can't see it will ever be with the white folks, i will never fit in, they will never allow me too, despite what the man I told you about - Aleixo, has said. I have no idea what will happen when Aleixo goes to his homeland to care for his family or whether I can actually accompany him as he wishes but I know that whatever he says the welcome will be it will be nothing compared to the companionship and peace I have found here over the last few days.

Gently Chenoa once again laid her hands upon Irisa's, she had no words of solace or knowledge to give, just to let Irisa feel the gratefulness and empathy she felt towards her.

Slowly, Irisa walked away, back to the hut she had shared with Aleixo knowing that their stay here was coming to a close and that she would have to face going back to the Governor's house and to then prepare for another long voyage. However much she loved being at sea and enveloping herself in the hipping waves and salty air, this was a journey she was dreading. Although the hold this time would be full of spices and tobacco and not slaves, she still felt she was heading towards more heartache and further away from her family and she felt queasy at the thought of it.

Chapter 32- The offer.

The following morning dawned bright and clear and there was even the beginning of the edge of crispiness to it that suggested it wouldn't be long before a change of season was upon them. They would no longer be grumblings about the heat and dust but rather the cold and wet. Some people just couldn't see the beauty in such changes, Irisa however was captivated by the thought of all the trees changing their deep green leaves for bright copper glistening throughout the woodland.

Aleixo was already packing up their few belongings, readying for their return. They had been asked to first visit with Sachem in his hut and they were both glad of the hospitality they had been shown. Irisa however felt the pull of leaving and was shocked at how close she had grown to these people in such a short space of time.

Irisas replaced her skin clothes for the western style dress she had been given by the governor and was fidgeting with herself as they made their way across the homestead. They came into the Sachems hut, the Sachem and Chieftess seated on high wooden seats, alongside Chenoa on a slightly less raised platform. Wyono indicated for them to sit on the brightly coloured woven rugs that had been spread onto the floor, and joined them as they made themselves comfortable.

The Sachem - Abooksiquin began to talk to wyono and indicated for him to pass this onto Aleixo and Irisa.

Wyono smiled at the two and began, ‘My father says Mother earth is starting to breathe her coldness into the air, there is a sharp crispness to the dawn. It is time for plants and animals to prepare for the big cold sleep and for those of us who remain to gather and prepare for our winter camp. He says he knows you feel it woman, you see Mother earth sprinkle her icy breath and soon we will be wrapped in frost mites. When this happens. We pack up our lives here and head deep into the forest to the winter camp, by the beginnings of the Rappahanock river where we will have some protection from the icy winds within the comfort of the tall pine trees. We are never found, we tell no soul where we are, we come to the white man's town to trade and we live well enough from it. You have shown how valuable your skill is, both of you have been a friend to our people like no other strangers have. We know too Aleixo that your woman’s life was like this before, before you took her away from it. We now offer you a chance to live it again, to stay, to live with us. We give you good Indian names and white men can no longer control you. You could have a life of peace. It will not be rich in coins such as Vasconcelos offers you but you will be rich in love and purpose and at one with the Earth.'

Aleixo glanced at Irisa and watched her closely as clear tears streamed down her serene face, but she said nothing in response and Aleixo continued, ' Abooksquin, Aleshanee, you honour us with your offer, we have not been as contented as we have been staying with you and your family here. We must however return to Vasconcelos to return the trade deal you have agreed to. I would need to find another way to send money to my family who do need coins to survive and know that they would be safe. May we be given time to consider? If we agree I worry it would be difficult to get away and we would not wish to put anyone at risk either back at the plantation or here at your settlement.'

'What you say boy, I understand, however let us consider danger. I will look for you in two weeks, then we will be moving to the deep forest, we will not be found, give this thought in your heart and head, not just for you but for the woman you have claimed to own and love. We would all benefit from your company boy.'

Irisa moved forward on her knees, seeking a blessing from Aleshanee, which she gave readily. She asked Irisa to stand and held her tightly when she did. 'You saved my life and my soul, there are not enough words in either language enough to give thanks for that.'

The pleasure was mine, I was able finally to use my gift for good and that felt wonderful, natural. I have felt welcomed, loved and accepted, I leave with reluctance and a heavy heart.'

Aleshanee smiled indulgently at her and whispered, 'Then return to us my dear, with or without this man.'

The Priest had been silent whilst Sachem and his wife had spoken, unusual for a man that always had an opinion and something to say. The group were about to leave the tent when he quietly interjected, ' Uhm, excuse me, may I speak Abooksiquin? I believe I have something to say.'

Having endured other white priests and vicars who had come to their lands to try and try and change their religion, dismissing it, ridiculing it even,

Abooksiquin was reluctant to let the man say anything, but he did come with the other two whom he now trusted implicitly, so he gave him the chance. He signalled to his son, one false word and the prophet would never again speak.

Irisa gently grabbed his arm and whispered,' Are you sure you wish to speak? I'm not sure what you have to say will be welcomed here Father, with the greatest respect.'

He roughly pushed Irisa's arm off his, 'Yes, yes- he stuttered- I do have something to say, if you would help me Wyono.'

Wyono studied the priest and nodded sagely. ' I will translate to my father but be wary of what you try to teach him, for if he dislikes it, you will die here.' Francisco stood nervously forward, 'I understand what will happen. I would still like to have my say, I appreciate you relating this to your father.'

'Great Sachem, I come from a world where even the religious are greedy, they hunger for power, for material things, for gold at their altars and nobles and the rich to worship in their churches. I do come from this, I have been this and I have felt that hunger. Much good it has ever done to me. That was why I decided to make this trip.I do not hold with the work of slavers, I do not believe in imprisoning one people to profit another and I do not believe that my god, your gods, Irisa's gods or any gods would think this right. I followed Aleixo and Irisa here after feeling sick with the gluttony of the church and wanted to witness what Irisa could or could not do.' he turned to her with a rueful smile, ' I am afraid my dear that I had little faith in what you said you could do. Then I witnessed you healing, I saw the darkness leave you and enter Aleshanee, I witnessed her release it and become healed and I fell to my knees and prayed to God, asked God if he knew these gifts could be given and I truly do believe I witnessed a miracle. I feel that whether our gods are one and the same, or they are as we believe, I can not deny what my own eyes witnessed and I know with absolute certainty that there is a presence in our world that protects the deserving, that can heal the poor and punish the wicked and I want to celebrate that! I want that to be in my heart when I think about how I myself shall live. Who am I to say that my way is better than yours? Since entering your home, I have found nothing but hospitality, I have watched as your people share everything they have and work together to gain for their community. I believe that this is the most blessed place, the most holy of places and even if I were to go back and build the biggest church in Christendom, it would still not hold a candle to this sanctuary. I ask this of you, if Irisa and Aleixo decide that this is where their life should be, please may I return with them? Not to try to instruct your people in the art of my religion but simply to come and live as one with you, to learn to be a good Indian,and work within your community?'

Irisa and Aleixo gasped at Francisco's speech, shock causing them to retreat into silence themselves. Abooksiquin stared at the priest and rose from his chair, towards Francisco, who fell to his knees as the chief approached him.

'I have no reason to trust your words, other than you have not tried to impose your religion on us whilst you were here. How do I trust you will not gain what knowledge you can about us, return to your greedy white merchants, betray our way of life, give them ammunition to gain the rest of our lands? What can you say to make me believe this is your heart speaking and not a plot?'

'I can only give you my word Sir and pray that it is enough. I understand if you can't accept me, I have long been unaccepted by others, I grow accustomed to it unfortunately.'

Abooksiquin started to walk back to his seat, but Irisa took the priest's hand and smiled. ' I can vouch for this man. I can tell you that you may not always agree with what he says, but I can feel that this man is pure of heart and is genuine in what he tells you. I believe that he, like me, is not enamoured by wealth and prosperity even if he once was. I believe we should all give him a second chance? I think we all deserve to live the life we feel is right in our hearts, if we can, please consider him.'

Aleshanee stood and made her way to her Chief, ' I believe him, I trust Irisa, allow him this Abooksiqun, my Chief, my love, for we owe these people much do we not?'

The chief sighed and laid his hand on Francisco's shoulder. He spoke fast in melodic Indian, Wyono translated, 'He says, yes priest man we give you a chance to be family and friend but do not betray me, you would not do well as his foe.'

Francisco's eyes glistened as he thanked the Chief again and again for the offer, and walked away towards Aleixo and Irisa to gather his belongings. They gathered their packs and began the long trip through the warm air that rustled with a cooling breeze. As they began to leave the settlement, Irisa tried not to look back, tried not to imagine what her life could be like here, how she could find peace and comfort. She felt that she and the priest would now have to await Aleixio's decision, although she still had Aleshanee's voice rattling around in her head, encouraging her to return to her spiritual home, without Aleixo and believed that the priest would do the same.

Aleixo carried a deep frown as he moved, his thoughts were clouded,troubled, he felt like he had been cut in two and that all the plans he had made before coming to the Indian settlement were not as secure as he believed they were. He knew in his heart what Irisa would want, he was just very unsure as to whether he could ignore the wants and needs of his own family and thoughts that Irisa would be selfish to make him make a choice swilled in his mind, whilst the other half of his head could not dismiss that he himself was the selfish one. He walked ahead and Irisa let him go, knowing that he was just as troubled as she was. They walked in silence.

Chapter 33- Walls.

Wyono walked with them to the edge of the summer lands, Irisa tried to absorb every moment, every smell, the fresh thick, oily green of the bluebells that scattered through the shorter grasses, she stroked her hands against the bark of the sassafras trees, the warmth of cinnamon filling her airways. She stopped to take some of the roots to make sassafras tea, securing it in her bag. It was as she walked through the bushy grey, green leaves of the sage plants and stopped that Father Fransisco came over to her.

'Don't be too hard on him Irisa, he has a difficult choice to make, he is struggling with the conflict in his head and his heart, let him have space, Wyono is with him.'

'I know father, I just fear what that will be, I can surely not compete with a mother's love.'

'It is not a competition my dear, I can see that he loves you but would you want him to love his family back home less? That would make him a very different man would it not? You may not have loved him at all then. Tell me what are you doing collecting all these leaves and plants? I have never worked with herbs although some back home did, they made pastes and teas to help the poor to heal.'

She passed him a sage leaf and modelled for him to screw it up in his hand and then smell it. 'In my home we would use this for food, it has such a rich aroma does it not? Some of the tribe women showed me how to use it to make teas that help people to sleep but it can also be used to help with seasickness and worms of the stomach. I thought it useful for our return to that wooden fortress, if that's what we have to do. I think my friends, Fugra and Amara, my fellow wise women, would like some to use for those on the plantation that they care for.

He gave her a genuine smile, probably the first one she'd seen from him, the first time she'd shown genuine pleasure in learning something new. 'I am over awed by your intelligence and all these things that you know, I apologise for my frankness, I have been brought up to believe that those peoples of your colour and country would have little or no knowledge, some people back home have discussed whether blacks can actually have any intelligence! If only they could see you here now, see the people we have just seen, they would think so differently don't you think?'

Irisa gave a deep sigh as she stood,' I wish I

could say yes father, but I feel for those that make their coin through selling others, they do not care whether we have intelligence or not, it serves them well to pretend we do not, that we are not as human as them.'

' I suppose you're right, let's hope with time it changes. For now let's worry about not tripping over all of these infernal bushes.'

They made their way companionably, allowing Wyono and Aleixo space and time as they all made their way towards the edge of the forest. All taking in the overwhelming beauty of the land, where the eagles soared high into the china blue sky in stark contrast to the ominous onyx black mountains,capped with the purest white snow.

They began to follow a brook, then a stream that eventually became the Rappahanock river. The water flowed and gurgled its way down, bubbling over the slick grey rock until it became a gentler flowing river. The glass-like surface, broken occasionally by the odd fish swimming up stream. She took in the grasslands that they now walked within, the swaying grass making her feel reminiscent of the sea that she loved.

Aleixo felt conflicted, unsure whether he felt

safer moving towards the apparent safety of the tobacco plantation or not. He had felt at ease with the indigenous folk but he knew as well that he had to get money to his mother and sisters and he could only do that by following Vasconcelos home, there was no one else to trust, even Pero. He knew people would make promises to his face, but he also knew that every mariner would be as deeply in need for money as he was, and they would take it as soon as they landed and it would never reach his family, there would be no way to find whoever took it, or indeed no way to prove it was his in the first place. He was anxious as to how Irisa would react when he shared these thoughts, he wondered whether there love was strong enough or whether she would be drawn to a life with the Algonquins and make a home for herself there, good lord maybe even with Father Francisco, who had amazed Aleixo with his speech back with Wyonos' family. He understood why Irisa felt so ill at ease at the plantation and with its household. God's breath, he was from those people and at times it made him wince at their thoughtlessness of others and how highly they valued themselves because of their white skin.

He sighed to himself, Irisa wasn't the only one

who suffered jibes and taunts, she presumed he was above it as he believed Irisa saw him as white, just like Vasconcelos and the mariners from England, but his coming from Portugal meant that he was far from light skinned, indeed he was swarthy with the darkest eyes, he did not fit in with the white and could only make himself a place in London as a lower working class man, a sailor or a wharfman. In Portugal he would make himself a Captain, he would sail the seas he loved, bringing more wealth and happiness to his family and he wanted that to include Irisa.

The whole group seemed lost in their own thoughts as they made their way to the edge of the land that the Governor had 'claimed' for himself, they began to see the fields of tobacco plants, the musky scent drifting on the air. Lost in their reverie, It was a few minutes before Irisa, Aleixo and Francisco realised that Wyono had stopped.

"Leave you here my friends, I hope you consider what my father said and return to us, they did not ask people to join us before, I think you would be family with us, think well on it.'

Aleixo smiled in return, ' We are honoured to have been asked by Wyono, we will look deep into our souls and hearts before we make a decision, but how will we contact you?.'

'Come to the edge of these lands, build a fire, let the smoke come to tell us you are coming home to us, we will find you.'

And then he was gone. Irisa felt her heart wrench as Aleixo felt his soar. The hideous trip filled with hate and violence would soon be over and life could begin, maybe he could even befriend Pero again, maybe once they were back on home soil, his old friend would lose the darkness within him and be grateful to be home, like Aleixo.

It was another hour of hiking across the plantation fields before they began to see the edge of the slave quarters. Aleixo carried on towards the big house to report to Vasconcelos and the Governor to share the response from the Algonquins and what they had agreed to trade. He only hoped that it would be enough to sate the greed of both the men he now had to face.

Irisa decided to stay behind in the slave village, trying to put off returning to the house and its pomposity and chose instead to spend time with Fugra and Amara. Aleixo knew that this meant she wanted to be with her friends to consider what the Chief offered and understood that she would not be able to rest until she had solidified and secured her thoughts, so kissed her lightly on the lips and walked towards the grounds of Bellewater.

Fugra and Amara were grinding herbs in their hut, making tisanes for the people who visited on a daily basis and for those too sick to leave their primitive beds. These the white folk deemed the most urgent for production of tobacco in the amounts they were growing was a relentless task and they needed healthy, working slaves. Oh they had no care for the health of those they worked to the bone, but they did value the tobacco they could cut and dry, so the women tried their best to make them comfortable, knowing that if they could not be made well, they would be 'moved on' which in reality meant being shot as they were then considered no use to anyone, shot without compunction, left in the dirt as they would any suffering beast of burden.

Irisa swept in and grabbed Amara by the waist, 'Oh my friend I have missed you!' I would have loved to share the moments of beauty I saw when we visited the Algonquins. They live just as we did back home, although of course it is not as warm here, but the land is bountiful with Mami wata- they say 'mother earth', whoever created this land is a magnificent God, this land is such a sight to behold, it is mesmerising!'

Amara gave a beaming smile back at Irisa, 'I would have loved to have been with you too. It has been so busy here though Irisa, Fugra and I have been run ragged. Now tell us, did you heal the Chieftess? Does she live?'

'I did manage to save her, by the gods it was not easy though! She was dying, passing into the other place, a snake had sunk its venom into her blood and it was on its way to stopping her heart beating and her soul leaving this plane. I tried with herbs but nothing worked, it is a snake I have not seen before, the locals call them 'Copperheads' and they are deadly, they have no cure for this so beware if you manage to get out into the savanna, I had to use my God gift to bring her back.'

Fugra bristled, ' You stupid girl! So now you have shared it with another, wonderful, we'll probably all burn together now! Oh praise the Gods you took that idiot white priest with you, it's a wonder they didn't burn you there and bring back your ashes! What are we to do now then?'

Irisa stayed calm and did not react to the anxiety and distress that Irisa could feel bustling beneath Fugras anger. 'Oh Fugra as soon as I touched

Aleshanee's, she sensed it, she told me that they worship other gods too and they believe in spirits and talk to their dead, just as we did, I was in no danger and am still not, in fact they welcomed me into their homes and hearts, Father Francisco has had a change of heart, now he has witnessed what can happen he believes it is a miracle, enough so that he will leave and live with the tribe if he can! I was able to use the monstrous to retrieve the Venom and to not hurt the Chieftess. We spent a long time chatting about the spirit world. They have women who help others give birth but for medics, they use a 'Kwiocosuk' he's a man that comunes with the spirits whilst in a trance but he also helps to look after the sick, it was he who asked them to reach out for help when he could not heal the Chieftess. They live in peace Fugra, peace! They only started fighting when these white people arrived by boats filled with angry men ready for a war and believing that they already owned this land and they could take what they wanted! People like the priest were trying to force them to become Chistians, calling them savages along with the black slaves they brought with them. They only take what they need from the land, sea, river and earth, they work together as a unit, raise their children as a group, they dance and laugh into the night just as we did in Allada. In all honesty I did not want to come back from there, although I knew I must, if we had not returned with a favourable trade deal we would have all been hunted and shot.'

'Well we are glad you have returned my girl, maybe you could help us to prepare some healing pastes, many have injured hands from cutting the tobacco and they will lead to infections if we do not treat them, it is dangerous to not be useful here'

Irisa smiled, 'I would be glad to, I have brought some herbs that I gathered with the Algonquins, they seem similar to some that we use back home, I'll show you what I have.'

Irisa reached into a large leather pouch and began to produce leaves and barks, Amara gave Irisa a tired smile, ' I too am glad to have my friend returned safe from an unknown place but I sense that you did not come here to assist us, Are you not needed back at the house? Come, sit, tell me what bothers you.' Amara continued to busy herself, making refreshing kirni tea for them both and they sat together on the floor, sipping at the hot, relaxing mix. Irisa relayed all that the naturals had told her and what they had offered to her and Aleixo.

'Well what does Aleixo say? Does he want to give up his world to live in one such as ours? He has spent his life trying to work for his mother and sisters Irisa, so they can continue to live in their own community. Can he so easily forget them my friend?'

'I don't know, I don't know! Oh the Gods I don't know He has not even spoken about it, we walked home in silence. I don't know if he is feeling guilty at the thought of leaving his family and starting a new life or if he has no intentions of ever giving it another thought. In my heart I had hoped he would be thinking it was a blessing to be able to live in peace and that you and Fugra could join us. I am distraught at the thought of having to leave and go to this European country and live like them, but I have no choice, at the end of the day the only reason I, or 'we are alive is because Aleixo owns me, and like his luggage and his coins he can take me wherever he wants, unless I were to run away and then he would have the right to shoot me! I keep trying to make a choice but do I truly have one? I don't think I do.'

Fugra laughed, 'Here you go with your silly dreams again! I can not leave this place, I am old, I am settled here and yes it can be a hell but I have a purpose and I am allowed to use my skills and they leave me well alone, our people that have no choice are here and they are relying on me to keep them and their children alive, I will not leave them and you should not ask me but I am happy for you to start a new life, wherever that may be. You are young, it is right for you, the Gods have willed it or we would not have come to this impasse.'

Amara looked at her feet, 'Irisa, you know I would do anything for you, I would, but the truth is that I have met someone, a kind house servant called Joshua, of course that's his given name here, he is caring and thoughtful and we hope to marry, other have done that here, among the servants. I will come if you insist but I have given this man my heart, just as you seem to have given yours to Aleixo.'

Irisa pulled Amara towards her, 'All I have ever wished for is that you have a happy life and find love, you are born to be a mother, we all saw that with Magra's little one, bless the Gods. I would not want you to make such a difficult choice, especially if you and Joshua have made promises to one another, they should be kept. I know Fugra needs the help even if she's too stubborn to admit it. You need to think about your own heart and do what is right for you.'

They held each other for a long time until Fugra

broke the silence and comfort. 'Come you two, we don't have all day for sentimentality, there are children out there, many with some kind of fever I can't get on top of, let's see if together we can stop them from passing to the other side.'

The three women filled linen cloths with supplies and made their way through the ever growing slave encampment. The first few hours sped past in a nightmarish trance, Irisa had no idea of the fever that had spread through the place since she had left. They saw child after child with the same symptoms, abed with a high fever and nothing the families were doing was helping, they were distressed and helpless. The women went to hut after hut administering teas and tisanes for those within and prayers to their Gods, to Mammy Wata to save the babes from making their way to the swiftly growing burial grounds where many tiny mounds sat stark and sad.

The sun glowered down on the women, exhausted by their work and sorrow at the four little ones that had not survived. They were sitting taking a moment on a small clearing when Aleixo found them. He had been with Father Francisco, helping the fathers dig graves for those they had hardly had time to get to know. Before he had time to speak to Irisa, Vasconcelos came stomping in, furious that he had to come looking for Aleixo when he couldn't locate him at Bellewater.

'Good God man, you look awful, what happened, did those damn savages attack you?'

Aleixo shook his head and for the first time broke the boundaries between classes and spoke harshly to his Captain. 'Savages! They are not the savages, we are! We are the fucking savages! They were nothing less than welcoming despite it being whites coming to them, the whites that have taken their land, spreading disease among their people. You really want to know why I look like this? Why dirt streaks my face and red eyes peer at you from it?' he pointed to the clearing in the distance ' I have been digging graves for fucking children, Children! Some but babies with no life lived at all. We did this! We brought disease to this island, these people have no protection from it, I might as well have killed them with my own damn hands, that is why I look like this!'

Vasconcelos frowned deeply, taken aback by the rebuke from a common man.

'Mind your filthy tongue and remember your place! I have taken good care of you and your own and

I do not expect the behaviour of a reprobate in return! I will allow your temper to cool. I know how hard it is to bury children, I had to do it with my own young son before we voyaged here. I wish no man that hurt whatever colour his skin but you must remember why we are here Aleixo. You are my first mate, you were paid to capture and transport these people here, you accepted that job and you will do it. The slaves we brought are not sick and it is not our place to judge how the Governor manages his workers. We only have a few days before he pays us and our only job is to keep alive those we brought, so use your bonus, your whore and get the job done! That fucking woman has got inside your head and I swear, if you do not tow the line, I will have her burnt as a witch on our return and have you tied up beside her!'

Irisa gently placed her hand on Aleixo's shoulder, her way of expressing 'enough now' and guided him away from the Captain, who was still shouting out to him, ' I will send Pero to help their foreman, they need to clean out their dwellings, we'd never run a ship this way, we'd all be dead. Tell the priest to stay a while with the families who have lost little ones.'

Despite Aleixo knowing that he meant well and

was trying to appease him as well as his own conscience, he could not help but despise the Captain, who even in his sympathy could not help but understand that the last thing these grieving people might want is a white man trying to convert them to christianity, saying strange prayers over their children.

In the end Aleixo was pleased to see that he was wrong about the priest's intentions. Father Francisco had been accepted by the community because despite his duties he did not try to convert the Africans, he listened to their prayers with them and then added his own. He had learnt and changed since being with the Algonquins and had begun to gain respect from the slaves when they heard the tale of his journey, could see his kindness and compassion. He sat with those struggling with loss, with a candle in comfortable silence. He fought for them to have a day to bury their loved ones, despite making him unpopular with the Governor. He had begun to see things for what they were, understanding that these people were not satan worshipping heathens, they were people worshipping their own Gods just as he did as a christian. Aleixo felt grateful for the comfort the priest gave to the grieving.

That night under the cover of darkness, the others who had not wanted their children buried under the Governors orders but with their own rites, Francisco returned with them as they gathered their little ones who had already been wrapped tightly in rough hessian- the only material they could have access to, they had taken the material the tobacco leaves had been wrapped in. The tradition was to bury their dead with the items they had used or treasured in this world, so they could have comfort in the next. There was fear among the slaves that if they could not bury their dead properly, their spirits would bother them in life. So the priest watched tearfully as they buried toys, simple cups and bowls for their beloved children.

Irisa sat uneasily in the hut with Fugra and Amara. She could not watch the burials a second time, she felt her heart would break, so she sat waiting for Aleixo's return.. He had taken himself off after his argument with the Captain and she knew that he would be considering what would happen next in his life and where his life would be.

Fugra had been boiling a pot of intsenga tea to give to weary parents as they returned. Many didn't take the offer of the calming tea, preferring their own brewed Mewengi banana beer to dull their senses. There was an unrest in the camp no, intensified by grief and sadness, turned to anger and resentment on top of the humiliation of being treated as animals. So intense was the feeling, it felt like a physical barrier had been erected between the camp and Bellewater. Irisa could sense it, forming, swirling and deepening. Trouble would come to this camp and she worried that much death would follow.

Chapter 34- A Souls Appeal.

It was a rapping on the door of Fugra'shut that pulled them out of the melancholy they all felt. Sipping hot camomile tea, Irisa called for the person to come in, thinking it to be Aleixo. It was a young man whom she had briefly seen up at Bellewater. Amara stood up and ran to him and he held her tightly, then gently moved her to his side.

Forgive me Amara but I am her only briefly, I am on an errand for the Governess, she would like to see you please Miss Irisa. She is quite distraught and says that only you can help her, will you come madam?'

'Well you can stop calling me Miss anything! My name is Irisa.'

Eyes cast down, the visitor nervously continued 'yes, Irisa.'

Amara went to his rescue, 'Oh Irisa stop giving him that attitude, this is the man I told you about, this is my Joshua.'

Irisa looked him up and down, clearly evaluating him and his intentions like a nervous father whose daughter is meeting her bequeathed for the first time.

'Well best you look after her my man or Fugra

will turn you into some foul; creature and I will send you to hell!"

'Irisa that's enough! This man has been kind and courteous to me, he has taken no imposition, you need to respect my choices as well as I respect yours, please there is no need to scare him to death to ensure he cares for me, he loves me well enough. I'm sorry Joshua, my friends are rather protective of me.'

He acknowledged with a slight of his head, 'It is ok my love, you did tell me that Irisa would give me hell, knowing she would send me to it if I hurt you tells me she has a great friend and protector in her and that can only be a good thing.'

That broke the ice and Irisa smiled at him, 'Well I'd better follow you to the house then or she'll send out a search party.'

Slowly Irisa followed Joshua to the large entrance hall, gazing into the shine of the brilliantly polished marble floors, the gold leaf glistening from the walls, she still could not believe that people dwelt in homes of this size and grandeur.

'You have true feelings for my friend then? She asked in a friendlier manner.

Joshua blushed red, 'I do, I will make her my wife when I am allowed. I am a household slave which means she'll have a better place to live, we will be happy together I think.'

'Mmm, well, Amara may well not have told you all that she has been through, our journey to this place has been long and hard, she has suffered greatly and I wish her only to be loved and happy now, she deserves nothing less. If that is your intention and I sense it is, I give you both my blessing Joshua.'

He smiled back bashfully, 'Thank you, that will mean so much to Amara, she was worried that you would not want her to stay.'

'I will miss her my whole heart, we have been together since we were children tumbling about in our village, but I would never stop her from reaching for her own dreams, love her well.'

Irisa was distracted by a movement from the corner of her eye, a door opened onto the entrance hall, Vasconcelos came out along with the Governor and to her horror, Pero. She turned away hoping to be missed but instantly Pero saw her and sidled up to her and Joshua.

'Ah look Governor, your house slave has found the witch! What's the rotten bitch been doing now?

The Governor looked from Pero to Irisa with a horrified and confused look on his half stunned face.

‘I was told she was not a witch! She’s been helping those bloody naturals so we can trade, she has been useful to us, but no, I will not tolerate witches in my household! Speak wench, are you what he says?’

Irisa stood her full height knowing how frightened the Governor was of witchcraft, she knew she could use it to her advantage. She walked slowly across the hall brushing past Pero until she faced the Governor.

‘As well you know I am proficient with the use of herbs and plants and using them to heal others, as I have with your wife and for your sake the Sanchems wife. I do not know if this is witchcraft, I certainly worship nothing evil. I am friendly with your christian do gooder, Father Francisco, maybe you should ask him?’ She took another few steps until she was sure that the Governor could feel her breath on his face, ‘ or, maybe I should try and commune with the spirit world, maybe I can find this devil you all believe in, Satan is he called? I could find him, use him, is that what you wish for, Governor?’ she curtsied and stepped back.

The Governor was incensed but wary of Irisa and bumbled his speech, ‘I, I, well I, you insolent hussy! How dare you bring the name of the evil one into my home! I could have you burnt for that.'

Irisa smiled, ' Sir, you were not as attentive as you should have, I do not do the things you accuse me of, I simply ask if that is what you would like me to try as you seem so convinced. This man- she pointed directly to Pero, is an evil and disturbed man, he takes pleasure in violence and harming others, especially if those others happen to be female, it suits him to spread such gossip.' Irisa stopped commenting further as Vasconcelos stepped forward, red with rage.

'Pero! You are a troublesome prick and you have been since you set foot on my ship. I know something of your life before and only because of that do I give leniency but I will not have this! We are in the company of the Governor and I will not have you behaving like a begrudged infant, nor will you band the word 'witch' around so freely! This is Aleixo's slave choice, they are a couple now and whether you like it or not, this is how it is to be. This woman helped us on the ship, she has helped many of her own kind and she has helped those we wish to trade with, do not rush to purge that! Now get back to the dock, there are goods to load ready for our return voyage, Go!'

He looked around and bowed to the Governor, 'I apologise for his impertinence, we know that Irisa is not a witch, how ridiculous is the idea that I would harbour one such as that! She is with one of us, I've never seen her worship her own gods, let alone devils!' he laughed sharply, encouraging a nervous laugh from the Governor in return.

'Oh yes, well of course, it's just that one can't be too careful, you know what it's like with these blacks, they worship all sorts you know! Woman, I apologise for my own superstitions that meant I have questioned your loyalty, go now with Joshua, my wife is anxious to see you.'

Irisa made her way slowly towards Anna's quarters, her heart conflicted as she marvelled at the luxuriousness of the furnishings whilst feeling slightly nauseous surrounded by so much wealth. As she neared the suite, she heard anxious pacing, small heels clicking on the wooden floor as she did so. Irisa knocked quietly on the door, 'It is Irisa, Miss, you wanted to see me?' she stepped back whilst awaiting a reply.

Hastily the door opened and Anna pulled Irisa inside, tears sprouting from her eyes, 'Oh thank the good lord! I had seen father Francisco return but I haven't seen you, oh Irisa I need your help, I can no longer remain here!'

Irisa frowned, 'What do you mean, that you can no longer stay in this room, this suite? I do not understand what you are asking of me? What has happened?'

Anna swept to the window seat bathed in the warm orange glow of the afternoon, she held her dainty white hands in her lap, staring down at them while she spoke. 'I have told you a little, I think, of how it is to be a woman and a wife here Irisa, I am trapped here with a man I can not love, my daughter is now destined to be used to make a fortuitous marriage to ensure he commands even more wealth. I will not make my daughter go through the damned heartache that I have had to, with no chance to follow even the smallest wishes or dreams unless it is convenient or prosperous for her husband. I have been writing in secret to my sister in Devon, back home in England, she has assured me that we would be welcome to live with her. Her husband passed this last year and she has a large property and a healthy allowance that she says she is happy to share! It is as if an angel came and saw our plight and gave us mercy!'

'If you have been offered a safe place to live then why would you need my help? I am glad you have a good sister, go to her.'

'Oh I wish it were that simple, The Governor would never let me leave believe me I have tried before. He would not stand the embarrassment, he would not survive it, he knows if I leave he will be exposed as the weak soul he really is. The only way that I can leave here with my daughter is if you help us escape on the Juniper when she leaves, I am begging you!'

Irisa was dumbfounded, 'How can I smuggle you aboard a ship? I apologise for the bluntness but you are rather obvious madame and along with your daughter, how could we disguise you ?'

'I have been thinking about it, maybe we could find a way to dress Rosa up as a boy for the ship and myself as a slave? There must be a way.'

'You are as white as a snowdrop Anna, how could you become a slave! There is nothing that would persuade me to try and pass the beautiful Miss Rosa off as a boy! A blackboy at that, wouldn't that look obvious to the Governor and surely he would notice your absence'

'Well I think not, at least for a while, I heard the Captain talking over your departure with one of the mariners, the tide is highest at the peak of the night at present, any disguise would only need to be good enough to help us sneak out at night fall, Lillabelle I have already spoken to, she is the one who attends me, she has agreed to say that Anna and I have caught a fever and he will leave us for most of the day, that gives plenty of time for the ship to sail and for us not to be found until the last moment.'

Irisa shook her head, 'I can see that you have really given this some thought, I truly do understand about wanting to escape, I understand in more ways than you could know, but I am sorry Anna, I just do not think it is possible.'

Anna moved towards Irisa and held her hands within hers, 'please will you at least give some thought to it, to how you may help another two women find freedom and happiness? Please Irisa? Is there no way you could use your gift to help us?'

Irisa stiffened at the mention of her God gift from the lips of this white woman. What did she think Irisa could do, kill everyone that got in the way? Protect her in some way? In any event whatever Anna might think, Irisa could see no logical reason for her to use her gift as she either left or escaped herself, she did not need to risk exposure of her gift to the whole plantation, she would be hunted down and burnt as a witch she was sure.

Anna stumbled over her words, knowing she had pushed Irisa away a little by mentioning what she had heard. 'I, I, oh Irisa I am sorry, I did not mention this to scare you or threaten you. I heard Vasconcelos bragging about it to the Governor. It sounds miraculous, I already knew you had skills but to save life, to grab onto the threads of life, that is indeed a miracle! I thought maybe if anything happened to Rosa, you could protect her, pretend I never mentioned it, I am just so desperate.'

'Indeed! If there were any way,~I would protect your daughter with my life, I have seen enough women ill used at men's hands. However, I can not do what you think I can, and I am angered that you are desperate enough to expose and endanger not just me, whom you call friend but also my friends who work as healers here and all those that they associate with! That is below you and selfish. My gift can be dangerous.'

Anna bowed her head, wringing her delicate porcelain hands together, 'I am again sorry Irisa, but you are right, I would consider anything to keep my daughter safe and to give both of us the chance to live a full and happy life, that is worth a risk is it not?'

Anna, I can make no other promise other than to think about it tomorrow but if I can not come up with a plan that I believe could absolutely work, then that will be the end to it as far as I am concerned, do you understand.'

Anna sank back into the window seat, deflated and a little tired that she had just been told off like a small child, by someone who she considered below her, but she no longer felt or believed that, she held onto a glimmer of hope. Irisa walked away, equally angry that she had been asked to engage in something as dangerous as this, something that if it went wrong could see her hanged. She still felt confused about her own decisions on whether to leave or not and did not feel she could keep it all in her head and her heart. She went off to re-visit Fugra and to find the space to pray to Takhar, God of justice, maybe he could guide her to what was right for all of them.

Chapter 35- Troubles.

It was as she was on her way to the slave quarter and Fugras hut that the seed of an idea was planted. Francisco, the priest had made his views quite plain to Irisa, that if he could make a choice it would be to stay and learn with the Indians, the Algonquins, but as far as anyone else but her and Aleixo were concerned, he was returning on the Juniper, along with one or two young boys who had shown an interest in learning and becoming a good christian, learning a new religion. These boys would be brought back to England to be cared for by the church, radicalised into angloism and then after a few years, returned to their own country, or where they were owned as a slave in order for them to then attempt to convert others within their own tribe into 'good christians' Could she work with Francisco? Could he be persuaded to help provide a potential escape route for Rosa at least? It would need time to work through, presuming he agreed but it gave her a glimmer of hope that it was possible. She knew also that she had to face the fact that Aleixo would have to know, even if it was just about Anna and Rosa, maybe she could give herself a little while longer to prevaricate about her own decision. Her heart and soul felt heavy and she had no idea how to progress the thoughts that flooded her mind.

Fugra was alone in the hut when she entered. ' Amara has gone to do the rounds for those who can't leave their beds. We're doing our best to keep them alive, but some are not strong enough to survive this sweating fever. You seem a weary child, what did the great madam want this time?'

'Oh Fugra you make her sound like a shrew! She is not so sharp but she did ask rather a lot, without realising what the consequences might be if we were found out.'

Irisa related all that she had discussed with Anna and then her thoughts that had niggled at her mind on her way to the hut. She finished with a deep sigh and turned her face towards Fugra.' For the first time, I truly do not know what to do. Whether to help her, whether to help myself, or must I go along with the flow of this life and accept that this is it, this is how it must be. At the end of the day I am just a woman, a slave, an owned piece of flesh, I am not sure I have the strength to be anything but that.'

Fugra came over to her, 'Well this calls for one thing, here, have this' she shoved a small cup of a foul smelling liquid towards her, with the smallest shavings of a root within the liquid. ‘ Why have you made me devil's claw tea? It’s vile!’

Fugra frowned at her, ‘Vile yes, but you need to commune with the gods, with the spirits, communicate with Mami wata for the earth, for Gu who can fix things, for Takhar, to see what is just and to visit Sama, heaven is not just for christians you know. Seek the answers that lay within your heart Irisa, this is the only way you can have clear thought. I will guard you, now drink, it is even worse if you wait until it is cold.’

Grimacing, Irisa gently sipped at the tea until she had emptied the small cup, then looking around the hut, she grabbed some blankets and made herself comfortable. She called to the gods to guide her, to give her the answers to what she must do, to keep her safe in the other realm, then she collapsed onto the blankets, deep in a drug induced haze from the devils claw.

Fugra pulled one of the rough cloth blankets over Irisa and kissed her gently on the forehead. ‘Travel well little one and return safe.’ With that Fugra continued mixing herbs and preparing tisanes, all the while keeping a watchful eye on Irisa as she fitfully slept.

Irisa slowly became aware of a gentle pink and purple light, she slowly opened her eyes and looked around her, sounds began to filter through as she watched the light change to yellows, oranges, then softening to hues of blue, small birds were chirping, trees began to appear and wave their leaves giving her a cooling breeze, she saw a woman sitting under the tree nursing a baby, as the woman turned she startled, the face, it couldn't be, but then there was that smile, it was her, herself staring back at herself. She barely had time to react before the light disappeared and grey light began to flood her eyes, she was in a port city, wearing western clothes, she was looking sadly towards the port, a small vessel was returning, sails down,as it moved towards her on an invisible sea, she realised that it was Aleixo's ship and he was not on it, Pero, head down shouting at the crew. Without knowing how, he appeared to dock in front of her and walked towards and then right through her, shouting, 'he's dead you bitch!' She gave a loud sob and the air vibrated and there she was again this time rushing two small children onto a ship she did recognise, the Juniper and above floated Thakur and Mami wata and they were pleased, they filled her soul with the light from the air and with a jolt she sat upright and felt disoriented until, in the gloom she heard a voice, Fugra, calling her back, she followed the voice in her head and then she opened her eyes fully and found herself laying on and within blankets, with Fugra leaning over her, smiling. 'Welcome back little one, I was worried I'd lost you for a minute there.'

'Fugra it was beautiful, the light was like being within sheets of silk, multiple colours and densities, flapping in a light breeze, I have a sense of peace now and I know what I must do, just not sure how yet.'

'It's not for the gods to give you lists of instructions my dear but to guide you to what is in your heart and to know your place in this world.'

'I will help Anna and Rosa, I can see a good outcome out of hardship, I can see happiness with the Algonquins and loss and tragedy if I head to the place they call Portugal. I will stay in Fugra, I will stay.'

Then Irisa let all her emotions go, she let them flood her mind, her heart, her soul, washing away the doubt, the guilt, leaving only hope and certainty.

Chapter 36- Resigned.

Fugra, Irisa and Amara talked late into the night, sharing ideas, talking them up and pulling them to shreds, so many things to try but eventually most hit a theoretical problem and they knew they would not work. As dawn's light filtered into the hut, saffron and warm, Irisa began to feel hope and that they had come up with the best solution for their problem, now all they had to do was manage the logistics of it all. Mostly they would rely on the one problem that they had previously sought to rectify - that mostly women were invisible, only good for domestic and conjugal rights.

As the chores of the morning started they set off in different directions - Irisa to seek out Father Francisco and Amara and Fugra to speak to the women in the slave camp. Irisa found the priest soon enough, since returning from the Algonquins, he had dedicated much of his time to helping the poorest and weakest of the children. She found him with a small girl, drawing pictures in the sand with sticks, the girl was giggling, a smile lighting up her filthy face.

Francisco looked up, 'Gods morning to you Irisa, See I have found a way to talk with the children even though we do not use the same words, drawing together we can share most of our thoughts and ideas, today we are drawing animals but I think Babiche here is laughing at my drawing of a snake.'He pointed to his scrawl in the dirt, saying snake, the child responded by pointing to hers and hissing, then pointing to his and holding her hand over her mouth as she giggled loudly.

'To me it seems you are also having fun father, does your god allow that?I thought him to be quite a stern god.'

'For once Irisa I care not what the lord thinks, only that I can sit here and for a few minutes this child is laughing and not worrying about what isn't in her belly. I would hope that any God would see that as benevolent.'

Irisa smiled at him, 'May we walk Francisco, I wish to talk to you candidly, but in private.'

'Well that makes it sound rather ominous, however I would trust you with my life now, so I am happy to hear anything you wish to speak of and of course, you have my word that it will not be shared.'

'Thankyou, I have to admit that although I have sat late into the night thinking about what I am about to say, I find myself nervous and hoping for your approval.'

'Continue my dear, you have my word I will listen with an open mind, remember I have seen the gift you possess and the power you can wield, I believe you to be an innate good soul and I doubt you could persuade me otherwise, whatever you are planning.'

Irisa went on to purvey all she knew about Anna and her relationship with the Governor and how she wanted help to get herself and her daughter away. Irisa was shocked that Francisco did not seem surprised by the idea, in fact the only thing he voiced was 'Well, not surprised he's a vile, greedy insular man.'

'Do you think you could help us? I was hoping that we could disguise Anna and Rosa as the young boy and man that you 'have chosen' to bring back to England to study, I have the disguise in hand, it will be late into the night when we leave, what do you think?'

'I do believe it could work! As long as we are swift getting onto the Juniper, most folk won't even notice, they'll be too busy with their own tasks, there is one small problem though my dear'

'You must be worried about what happens if we

are caught, I will do all I can to ensure that doesn't happen of course.'

'No, it is not that, I am now unconcerned by these peoples opinions, I no longer wish for a lavish church and followers to boost my morale, it is because I too had decided to stay with the Algonquins.'

'Ah, now that is a problem, I don't know how else we can get them aboard the ship.I will think again.' she began to bite her lips with her teeth, anxiety pouring out of her in waves.

'No Irisa, you misunderstand me, I still intend to stay with the Algonquins, we will just have to weave our way around it. I think we should go ahead and disguise them with me, we will board the ship as early as we can, get them out of sight, a safe place and then I will unboard the Juniper and make my journey towards the Indians.'

'Oh Father I can not thank you enough, I know Anna and Rosa will be grateful. Once they land in England, they know how to head to Anna's sister and safety.'

'If there is anything else you wish me to do, just name it, we are in this together now.'

Irisa faced Francisco straight into his eyes, as she shed light upon the dark side of the plan, unsure whether this would be a deal breaker.

'You have seen my gift Father, you know what that gift can do, well there is one person we will be directing that god gift to and that is a man named Pero, have you met him?'

'Sadly, yes, I have had that misfortune, I also remember how he treated your fellow villagers on our journey, made me feel sick to my stomach.' he shook his head in bewilderment. 'I do not understand that man but I think I can say with some certainty that he will be residing in hell when he passes from this life.'

'I think that we are in agreement. I have seen into his soul, he can not see past the revenge he seeks from every person with a darker skin tone than him. I know he will be the one to cause trouble, I can't explain it but I have seen it. He will alert Vasconcelos and they will return to this Island, then we will all hang and I will certainly be burnt alive, so my aim is to remove Pero from the situation. I am not sure how comfortable you are with that?'

'If you are asking me to kill Pero, I do not think I could do that, call me a coward but if you are suggesting using your gift of the darkness to hinder him or end him, I would not stand in the way and I would not be the one to judge you.'

‘I have options, I can either inflict the darkness upon him, so he is constantly bewildered and besieged by them, or I could put an end to the man who every day commits acts of cruelty and who seems to thrive upon it.’

Francisco nodded his head sagely, ‘I will leave that decision to you, without fear or judgement. Will we talk again before we put this plan into action?’

‘Yes, we will, I need to speak to Anna and Rosa and of course Aleixo, he does not know of my decision to stay and I owe him much, he at least needs to hear the truth so he can then make his own choice of where his path takes him.

Irisa walked away leaving Francisco thinking deeply on what he had been told. He was glad to think that in saving himself he could also be part of saving others and he would do anything for the girl whose God gift had changed his entire world.

Chapter 36-Resigned

Fugra and Amara were completing two tasks as one, going door to door, checking who needed any treatment, had those who were ill recovered or worsened but also sharing as much of Irisa's plan as was safe and to let them know they would be helping the Governor's wife and daughter. Many of the women felt pity for Anna and the child, despite their own dire circumstances, they knew they could make some small choices and they got to work beside the children they loved, teaching them to love the land, to believe in the world of God during the day and to worship the old ways deep into the night. Fugra felt sure they would help and it didn't put them at any risk either, which was why she had no compunction about asking for their favour.

Amara tapped lightly on the next hut door, wary of waking the little ones she knew were within, they had been battling a fever for the past few days and their mother had slept fitfully beside them praying to mami Wata to keep their spirits alive.

A dishevelled woman answered the door, 'oh Amara,Ashkuruk, thank the lord, do you have any more Umckaloabo? I fear the fever is in his chest now.'

Amara walked in and began rummaging in the small leather bag for the root she needed. 'I have a small piece left, we can grate this and make a tea, boil some water and we will try and make him comfortable. While water was collected, Fugra wiped the small boy's sweaty body with the cleanest rag she could find, propped him up on pillows and together they began to make the tea. Whilst they bustled around the hut, Fugra informed them of Irisa's plan to save Anna and Rosa and they wanted the help of all the women they could find.'

'Before you start regaling me with tales of what will happen to you if you are caught, let me assure you, you won't be, even if they knew they'd been helped there would be no evidence as to whom it might be and they cannot kill the whole group of workers on the plantation. All we ask is that we have any hair that has come out when you brush your hair, or when you cut one anothers, we need it to fashion two wigs of our natural hair to cover theirs, could you do that?'

'I'd be glad too, that pompous governor is an entitled pig and he treats his family no better than he treats his animals or even his slaves! I'd do just about anything to make sure no woman has to put up with that man!'

That's how the facts were received by the majority of the women they visited, by the end of the day they had a fine sack full of shavings and some women had taken their head to their scalp to help. No one questioned it, it was so damn hot in the tobacco fields that many women and men shaved their heads to get some relief from the heat and at times fleas.

Amara sent word to Irisa through Joshua that another morning and they would have enough to start the headpieces, the search for freedom had begun.

Chapter 37- Choices.

Wyono approached the grounds of the big house named Bellewater with trepidation. He did not like the majority of those that lived within the house and every time he visited he wanted to try and free the slave population. He hated the sense of entitlement these white men seemed to have over land that had belonged to the Indians for centuries.

Vasconcelos and Aleixo came out of the house to meet him.

'Kwey! I am happy to see you both, I have brought the last of the beaver pelts, I believe you are sailing soon?'

Vasconcelos smiled, yes we head back to our own country where the air won't fry or freeze us as it does here thank the Lord. I am grateful for the pelts, they will fetch a good price back home, I believe I say' Meegwetch' - he gave a proud smile, - your Irisa taught me Aleixo, quite the woman isn't she!'

Wyono laughed, indeed, Megwetch - thank you. Irisa listens well, you are indeed a lucky man.'

Aleixo smiled hesitantly, he loved Irisa to his core but she had been different of late, less attentive, he had put much of it down to her worrying about missing Fugra and Amara when they sailed on the Juniper, but he had an underlying malaise that there was something else happening that he could not voice.

'Well I wish you a good journey, shall we go to the stores? I have left the pelt there.'

The three walked off to do business. Irisa had been sitting with Anna and Rosa and absentmindedly gazing through the window. She had seen Wyono approach the house and saw he was not alone, she would try to catch him on his way out.

The three were sat with a small bowl of soot and two squares of muslin, scrubbing them with soot stained hands. Irisa looked up. 'These are almost done, let's get cleaned up, I have to try and catch Wyono, then I will find Fugra, I can take the squares to them and Amara will fashion them into wigs as best she can, they must be ready for two nights time when we believe the ship will sail. Let's hide this soot, I am going to add some oil to it and we will use this to change the colour of your faces and hands, everything else we can cover. We have a lot to thank Francisco for.'

Anna beamed, indeed we do, imagine Rosa we will be living at peace and freely with my sister, I can hardly believe it!.'

'Mamma it is my biggest dream to be with them but do you believe father will forgive us for leaving him in this way?'

'Oh Rosa you have a heart that is far too kind. Your father once had a sweet side to him and I will always be grateful for you having come from our love but he has been a mean, greedy and cruel man for many years now and I can no longer believe he will change. We have one chance to make an escape, this won't happen again, so we have to think just of ourselves now and make sure it works. Your Aunt has already spoken to a lawyer and divorce proceedings are beginning to be put into place. The minute we land in England they will be finalised. By the time your father realises what has happened he will be powerless to do anything about it and he can continue to treat people like animals without us having to be a part of it.

Rosa laid her head in her mothers lap. 'I know in my heart this is true Mamma but it is all rather terrifying is it not?'

Irisa held her hand gently. 'You will not be alone, you will be with other slaves who are going back to help the Captain with his ship and Aleixo will be there to keep you safe. You will have nothing to fear once you are away, I promise Rosa, I have spoken to my gods and they are pleased with my decision to help you, they will ensure that your sea voyage will be as kind to you as possible, they will look after you too.'

Rosa smiled and quietly went back to cleaning her hands. 'I'll help you hide this stuff Irisa, then you can go watch for the Indian man.' Irisa nodded and together they quickly finished their task.

*****

Wyono, Vasconcelos and Aleixo were drinking small beer, leaning on the barrels that would be loaded onto the ship in the morning. The store was full of provisions for the journey, thankfully more than on the journey to the middle passage, also full of crops and pelts and may other goods that could be sold to make a profit back home, stores of sassafras, herbs, tobacco, all the scents mingling together were not unpleasant to the men.

'I have been happy to know you Aleixo, I will miss your company when you have left, and Irisa's.'

'She will miss yours too, she was fond of your home, It was similar to the village that she came from, that I stole her from.' He looked sadly down at his drink, Vasconcelos jumped in,

'For Gods' sake man, we are slavers! That's why we came all this fucking way, it's a bit late now to feel guilt for one slave, in fact the one you own! She will be a good distraction on the return journey and you can use her how you will back in Portugal, you should have a smile from ear to ear about what you're going to do to her.'

'I can not think of her in that way anymore, she is not a slave to me.'

'Well she will be when you land in Portugal and with all the inquisitions you will have to watch she does not try and heal everyone in your damn town, or they'll start crying witch, you know how it is.'

'I will not put her in danger, I know the reality of what I have done, I just no longer feel comfortable with it, I shall be glad to go back to fishing in my village.'

'Hmm, well best you speak to your friend Pero then, he seems to love slaving, he's already asked to accompany me on my next trip! I'm not sure I want him, he's a liability and a bit of a loose cannon, he cost me with his violence, he spoiled more than one slave!'

'Pero is troubled, you know why, you have heard our story. We both thought it would bring us a sense of revenge for what was done to us, coming on this voyage, for me it has turned my stomach, for him, I don't know, he is not the same person. I think you are right to not trust him. I have however enjoyed spending time with your Allgonquian tribe Wyono, I learnt so much whilst I was there and I think I leave a little piece of my heart in your home.'

Wyono nodded, he knew he could not renew his offer to Aleixo for him and Irisa to come and live with them, not in front of Vasconcelos, it would be disastrous but he felt sure that Aleixo would know that it still held.

'I appreciate that and count you as a friend, Aleixo. May I say my farewells to Irisa before I go?'

'Yes of course I will go and find her, finish your beer.'

Alexio didn't have far to go, Irisa was then walking through the gardens, she had grown impatient waiting to find Wyono and was fearful of missing him if she watched from the window.

'Ahh there's my beautiful woman, I was coming to find you, Wyono wants to talk to you, to say farewell. I think he is sad we are leaving. I have to sort out these pelts with Vasconcelos, shall I send Wyono to the gardens?'

‘Oh please do, I have to ask him about a plant I have seen growing here, I have been collecting some cuttings for the ship. I need his advice.’

Irisa stayed where she was and Aleixo sent Wyono to her. They walked through the banks of roses. ‘You need my advice on a plant? Asked Wyono curiously, he knew that Irisa had a far superior knowledge of plants than he, so he knew she actually wanted to discuss something else. He grinned at her.

‘It’s not funny, I couldn’t think of anything else to say. I don’t want them to become suspicious.’

‘Why would they think it suspicious that we say goodbye?’

‘Not of that, Aleixo knows that I have been having doubts about travelling back on the Juniper. I have given this a lot of thought I have communed with my gods and I know that the only thing I can do is to come to your tribe and live with you, if you will have me? I can not bear the thought of the European lifestyle Aleixo so wants me to be part of, it is not me. If I go, I sensed tragedy for Aleixo and I would not have that either.’

Wyono frowned, ‘Our offer was genuine, I am glad you have chosen to live a natural life and to commune with the earth and sea, I just worry that we have little time left to make a plan to get you out of here. They sail two nights from now.'

'They do and there is much I have to tell you that will also be happening that night, it is not just myself that we are trying to save - oh and Father Francisco would also like to accompany us.'

As they walked slowly between the plants, Irisa tried to disclose as much as she could with Wyono, by the end of her tale, he had thought about what he should do.

'I will return to my people now, You and the priest must try to get to the edge of the forest the night they sail, without being seen, then I will meet you there with some of the men, we will then hide you and our camp will move deep into the forest. I can not be part of your plan to help the governor's wife. As much as I understand, my father, he would not like this.'

'No I can imagine he would not be able to sympathise with them, but I will help them, once they are on the ship, father Francisco will return to me and then we will both make our way to the forest. There will be much to distract everyone as the ship leaves and it will be some time before they realise that Anna and Rosa have left. Anna plans to leave a letter with

Joshua, who will place it somewhere obvious for him to read when the ship is out of sight, they will not search for the women then.'

'What does Aleixo feel about this? He gave no indication just now that he knew about your decision.'

'I have yet to tell him, I can not have my mind changed but I don't want me to be his focus, I am going to tell him the night the ship is sailing and pray that he does not give me up to the authorities. Will you promise to be there Wyono? I can hardly believe it will happen. I need the safety and simple life with your community where I can still have a purpose as a wise woman.'

'I will be there, you do not have to doubt that. I would ask you to tell Aleixo what you have decided, his heart is full for you and it will be hard for him to take,'

'I'll think about it, thank you Wyono, I owe you my life.'

'You saved my mothers it is only fair. Now let us bid farewell as friends, we are being observed and we need to make it seem that we will not see one another again.'

Wyono held her hands and Irisa lowered her head with tears in her eyes, then he simply walked away. It did not take much effort for Irisa to cry then, her head and heart were full of the consequences of her decisions.

Aleixo, who had been their observer, came over to Irisa and put his arm around her. 'Ahh don't cry my love, we have learnt so much from them that we can use back in Portugal to work on our own land and how to better fish the water where we will live. I noticed that you did not ask about the plant? Did you not need to know about that?'

Irisa felt herself still, he was suspicious but he didn't know what for, she would have to be careful. 'To be honest my love, I think my emotions got the better of me, I felt so overcome with sadness, I didn't even think about the plant.'

Aleixo held her closer and she tried to contain her guilt as they walked back together to the house.

Chapter 38 - Honour, Duty and Lies.

Irisa had tried but failed to take herself away from Aleixo the night before, every time she tried to leave there was something else he wanted to tell her about his homeland or the journey and how different this one would be. She knew that he felt in his heart something was not quite right, so she stayed and feigned interest in his homeland tales and waited until the morning. The madness of preparing the ship for a long voyage was now in full swing, there were repairs, loading, men working the rigging and plenty of arguments and disagreements that Aleixo had to calm down.He was so busy during the day she knew she would not see him until the evening meal, giving her time to put things in place for the following night when they would all leave.

Her first stop was to Amara and Fugra. Fugra was prepping bandages and medicines that would be taken onto the ship, Amara was sewing , her hand filthy. She had finished one 'wig' and was well on the way to finishing the slightly smaller one for Rosa. Amara held up her work to Irisa. 'They are not perfect by any means, but in the dark, maybe with a scarf or headband? Do you think they'll work?'

'Oh Amara, it's perfect! 'She turned the wig in her hands. They had braided the African curls into columns and sewn them onto the fabric that had been stained black with the soot mix. From a distance it did look like a black woman's head of hair. ' I think they'll work a treat! I've got clean servants' clothes for them to wear and Aleixo will hide more of their own on the ship.'

Fugra interrupted sharply' 'Does he know this yet? Have you actually told that poor boy anything?'

'I, I have not, Fugra, I don't know how to start the conversation.I am worried that if I tell him he will alert Vasconcelos to the plan to help Anna and Rosa and that he will then stop Fransisco and myself from going to the Algonquins.'

'Has he forced you into anything you did not want to do yet? Has he betrayed you in any way? I wholeheartedly agree with what you are choosing to do or I would not be helping but this is a decision that affects him too, you must tell him, if you trust him, tell him.'

Irisa's face began to wet with tears as they streaked down her face. ' I know what you say is true Fugra, it is just once I have said it, that is the end.'

'Do you have doubts about staying? Do you

think it would be better to leave?'

'No, no I believe my decision is right for me, I can not change it now.'

'Then go to him and make him understand why you do this, that he can stay too, he does not have to leave, it is worth a try is it not.'

Irisa nodded her head and made her way to the door. I'll be back later to collect them both, I can't thank you enough Amara. Irisa swept out of the door and made her way down to the port.

She was exhausted by the time she reached it, it had been some distance from the house. Aleixo had just left the ship to check some of the goods port side and spotted her form as she slumped down on one of the barrels.

'What on earth are you doing here Irisa, are you ok, you look pale?'

'I just wanted to see what all the fuss was about, now I can see, it's rather chaotic isn't it?'

He smiled, 'You get used to it after a while, once everything is on, it makes more sense. Here take some of this.' He handed her his hip flask and she took a long swig.

'Oh that's better, I was so dry. Aleixo I know that you are terribly busy but there is something I want to discuss with you, but I need to do it where there is no chance of someone hearing us, could we take a walk along the shore?'

'Just give me a minute and yes of course.'

He shouted to one of the mariners, gave him instructions and returned to Irisa.

'Come then, let's have this walk, it will be the last chance we have here, but when you are at my home, in the summer the sand is sometimes too hot to walk on! You will love it!.'

She smiled up at him, held the hand he had put out to her and they started to walk through the very edge of the warm water.

'Aleixo, I have come to be involved in something that I need to tell you about, there is much to this tale I'm afraid, so please, listen until I have finished. There will be times when you will want to shout or to stop me, but I beg you to let me tell it all as a whole, then, when I have finished you can ask me anything you want and I will answer honestly. Can you agree to that?'

Aleixo frowned at her, it was unlike her to be so serious, he had known that something was coming, now it was here he was unsure if he wanted to hear it.

'I will try my utmost Irisa to hear what you have

to say, please just tell me what's going on, I know something has been keeping you preoccupied and I need to know what that is.'

They walked through the water, around rocky pools and eventually sat on the glittering sand beneath a wide tree, as Irisa shared how she had been asked by Anna to help her escape and that Francisco had agreed to help, although he had decided to stay with the Algonquins so would unboard the ship after helping the governor's wife and daughter. At times, she could see him flinch at a particular statement, she was frightened of his reaction to her decision about Pero and she felt him recoil from her as she spoke. Eventually, in tears and afraid, she stopped talking. There was silence and the silence was bigger than the sky, deeper than the earth, hotter than fire and colder than the deepest water. It felt like eternity had passed until Aleixo spoke.

'You planned all this behind my back?'

'Not behind your back, at first I was frightened that you wouldn't help Anna and Rosa, I know you are not a fan of the Governor but did not think you would go as far as helping his wife and daughter to escape. I have to protect them for as long as I can.'

'But you know, as does Amara, Fugra, Father

Francisco and I presume Wyono!' anger began to drift from him, she could sense it and so could her God gift, the darkness was beginning to spike as its rotten souls smelt the essence of his anger.

'You are right to be angry,Aleixo, but time is short now. Tomorrow night there will be a blood moon as we are ready to set sail. We will bring Anna and Rosa with Father Francisco onto the ship and then help him to remove himself from the other side. Can I count on your discretion? Will you help? Can I trust you to protect Anna and Rosa on the ship? Once they land, their family will be waiting to take them away to safety.'

'Of course you can. I am angry at not being consulted but I would not see any innocent woman hurt,you know that, but, wait a minute, you said 'will *you* protect them.' why aren't you the one saying you will protect them, you'd be more effective, if Pero finds them in this all consuming angry mood he has been in, he'll kill them. Wait it still doesn't answer why you would ask me to protect them, you, you aren't coming are you! You are going to leave me and stay with the Algonquins! Please Irisa this is madness, I can give you such a good life, we will be happy together, you need not work, you can care for the house, you will love my family. I beg you not to do this.'

He was standing now, crying deeply as was she, she put her hand out to him and he pushed it away. 'I don't understand what I have done that is so wrong to you? All I have ever done is try to save you, from the moment I saw you.'

'I know that Aleixo, I know that you have love for me, but it has come from a place of invasion, of ownership and no, there has been no violence, you have not forced me into acts that most slaves have to perform, but I need to live my life as its best for me, all of me and that place is with the Algonquins, I can never get back to my home, that is your fault and the fault of all those on the Juniper, but I can be in a place where I can be with people who think like me, live like I did, worship like I did and I can not be untrue to myself, I have to be the one to make the choice, I am begging you to let me go. If however you would just come with us, we could be our own family here, living off the land, no wars, no class, no prejudice, it would be perfect. It is not that I do not love you, but I can not become a European, I won't. Please Aleixo, it is not just my life at stake, please.'

'You have ripped out my heart, but I would never betray you. I will help with getting Anna and

Rosa away from this self-entitled pig, I will even help you and Francisco get to the Algonquians but know that you have broken me.'

'I am sorry Aleixo, I had held onto the hope that you enjoyed the company of the Algonquins and admired how they lived, I thought you would accept their invitation for my sake and for yours.'

'And I would, in a heartbeat if it were not for the fact that I have family who are relying on me, who could die if I do not return with the money I have earnt from this satanic trip. I will never step onto another slave ship in my life. I am sorry Irisa, I can not let family down, it would kill me. However if there is ever a chance I can make my way back to you, I will.'

Irisa began to speak but held herself back, anything she added now would be cruel and would torment Aleixo so she swallowed her words and began a long slow walk back to Bellewater, stopping several times along the way to regroup and allow herself time to process what she had just told Aleixo. It felt like an eternity on that long walk back to the house. And so it was nearly dusk by the time she arrived dirty and dishevelled at the house. She was startled by the way the house was lit up and several carriages were dropping off couples dressed in the most elaborate clothes. She made her way to the servants entrance, and snuck in through the door. The kitchen was chaotic although it smelt divine. People were rushing to and fro and there was much excitement in the air. She bumped into Joshua who was then going through to the main house. 'My goodness mam where have you been? They have been looking all over the place for you.'

'I've been walking Joshua, what's going on?'

'Well seeing as it's your last day and all, the Governor decided to have him a party, you should be in there with Aleixo, he wants to show you off like a gem he found, he's been back for a while now' Joshua laughed. 'Best we get you cleaned up right quick, hey Miriam, come help this girl get right.'

Miriam- one of the maids helped sneak Irisa upstairs, get dressed, wiped her face, swept up her tight curls and brought her down again. Irisa walked into the dining room, she had just caught Aleixo's attention when the Governor grabbed her arm,

'Ahh here she is everyone, the one that healed Sachem's wife!' She was quickly enveloped with 'oohs' and ahhs' and too many questions to answer. She felt herself swirl with dizziness and promptly passed out.

She came too and found herself lying on Anna's

bed, with Anna watching anxiously over her. She tried to sit up but still felt a remnant of dizziness, Anna passed her a small cup of water and she sipped it gently.

'Oh now I feel like an idiot! I walked all the way from the port, without eating or drinking, walked into your party and made a complete fool of myself. I'm so sorry Anna.'

'You owe no apology to anyone. I did worry where you were though, thought something may have gone wrong.'

'Well it very nearly did. I knew I would have to tell Aleixo I owe him too much to just leave. I told him everything, I had to, I trust him. I knew he would be hurt and angry but I completely underestimated how he feels.'

'Oh Irisa any fool can see he loves you, can he bring himself to stay? Will he tell anyone, is our plan off? '

'No Anna, the plan is still on, thank the Gods! He will protect you and Rosa at sea,but he will not stay, he says he has to be true to his family. I told him we could stay here and be a family but he feels he owes it to his mother to return to her with the money from this trip. He says he will never set foot on another slaver ship though so he has learnt from that and he did say if ever there was a way to return to me, then he would but I don't see how. I have to think of myself from now on and how to protect the ones that I love.'

'Oh Irisa you are giving up so much for Rosa and I, will he help the priest as well? He has been the only one that has stood up to the Governor, I didn't expect that when he first showed up!'

'Me neither, I was not enamoured by him on the voyage out here but now I class him as a friend. He has a good heart and he is even kinder now he understands that his role is to help people whatever religion they embrace. I think he will become a wise elder over time.'

'Well I think you should lay here as long as you need, we do not know what fate will hold for us tomorrow, or whether we will all get away or not, but we are going to spend every minute of tomorrow trying, so rest now my friend, I thank my own god for bringing you to us.'

Exhausted, Irisa quickly drifted back to sleep. Although it was anything but restful. The darkness containing the monstrous was thinning, they could feel her need to use them and her need prodded them awake, filling her dreams with their vengeance and hostility, seducing her with their power and how she could use it, how she could extend its use. The monstrous were hungry for souls and they could sense those around them that were as corrupt and rotten as a piece of rotten flesh. Irisa tossed, turned and moaned in her slumber.

Chapter 39- Justice?

The following morning, as the soft light pierced the lacy curtains, Irisa was awoken by a loud banging and crashing around her. She was a little dazed and then remembered she was in Anna's bed. Anna was moving around the room at pace gathering items from draws and stuffing them into cases.

Irisa sat up, rubbed her eyes and shouted 'Stop! What on earth are you doing?'

'Well it is tonight we are leaving is it not? Rosa and I will need clothes for the journey and our toiletries and.'

'Stop Anna'

Anna sighed and sat on the bed, Irisa swept her legs round and placed an arm around her new found friend. 'You are escaping dressed as a slave, a slave who is accompanying a clergyman. You can not go on with cases! What will they think? Aleixo has agreed to take some linen bags with clothes in so that once and only once it is safe you can change into them for the remainder of the journey. It will not be pleasant, there will be smell, illness, sickness and you will be dirty and unwashed for most of it, you knew this Anna, you have to make this sacrifice to get safely away, you can not leave as the governor's wife and daughter that’s why we have gone to all this trouble to disguise you tonight.’

‘Oh I do know all of this but it does not seem to have stopped me from panicking and trying to take all the things I love, or so that Rosa would find comforting.’

‘Rosa thinks she is on a pirate adventure, she will endure it, she is more intelligent and stronger than you give her credit for. She will be well fed and protected, once you are safe with relatives, you will have all these beautiful things again. You need to think, do you prefer these ‘fanciful trinkets’ or the freedom to live as you choose for you and your daughter.’

‘Oh I am being silly, all the same I am anxious and I think it best that I stay away from the Governor for as long as possible today,I do not wish for him to notice anything is wrong.’

Irisa left Anna to decide on the basic essentials for her and Rosa, saying she would return within the hour to ensure the goods were given to Aleixo and put onboard the ship, Irisa just had to leave them in the stores.

Irisa firstly made her way to Fugra and Amara,

she was going to miss seeing them daily but at least she was staying where she would see them, not half way across the globe. There were tears and laughter and promises made to keep a wise woman eye out for each other. Irisa promised that she would visit every summer when the camp moved closer to the edge of the forest and Amara and Fugra promised that they would get a message to her if they needed any help, Joshua would be a reliable go between.

All three found there was too much to say and not enough time, they were reminiscent of their time in Allada, laughed at how Fugra told them off as children, how they loved their homeland and family and longed for it still, how frightened they had been when the raiders came and took them, how they thought they might die in the filthy wooden hut where they were cut in order be good whores and slaves, how the journey killed so many of their villagers, how they were treated like scum when they reached the tobacco plantation, but also how their strength as women, together helped them to find a better position in their lives, how they put themselves forward in order to save themselves and how they were keeping strong and still helping other women now. They had been through so much, lost so much hope, shared so much despair and then built themselves up again to feel strong and in control of their own destinies. They hugged tightly and wiped their tears as Irisa left them to instigate the plot to save two women as trapped as they had been.

Irisa ferried the newly made wigs to Rosa's room, where she felt there was less chance of anything being searched, then took the cloth bags to the stores and hid them behind the rum barrels. She slunk down onto the floor, the adrenaline flooding her body, she knew this was going to be one of the most difficult things she had tried to do in her life but she had determination and the Gods on her side. She heard light footsteps and anxiously turned, only to see Francisco coming towards her.

'Good morning Irisa, I thought I might find you here or with the Governor's wife. Is everything in place for tonight?'

Yes Father indeed it is, I have taken the whigs and the servants' clothes to Anna and Rosa, they will be ready after supper, so we can get them on and then make sure you have time to get off before they sail. We will have the cover of more darkness once the blood moon appears. Aleixo is not happy but he has agreed to help and he will protect them on the journey back to Europe.'

'Mmm, that is good Irisa, I had faith that he would help, where does that leave you both? Is he going to return to the shore too?'

'I'm afraid he is a loyal man and that means his first loyalty is to his family and not to he and I. I however know I have to come to the Indigenous peoples with you Father, we will escape together once the ship has left its moorings. If anyone tries to stop us then I have my God gift to fall back on as you know.'

'Oh you do, do you! You fucking witch!' Pero staggered to the stores, obviously out of his cups but seething with hatred. 'I've warned them since we captured you and your fucking people that you were an evil bitch that worshipped satan and now look! I see I am proved right and not only that you have seduced a man of the cloth to help you reek some evil plan! '

'You stupid man- Father Francisco replied with venom,' This woman has not seduced me! It has been working with vile idiots like you that has changed my mind, not an innocent woman with a heart better than you could ever hope to have. Cease your prattle you fool!'

‘Oh Father I will! But not before I have prattled on to Vasconcelos! Let’s see what he thinks of a plan to steal the Governor's wife and daughter! You will be hanged along with this bitch and I will spit on you as you burn!’

Pero ran at Irisa and grabbed her by the throat, his face reddening as he grabbed harder and began to take the breath from her lungs. The priest desperately tried to prise Pero’s hands from irisa’s throat but he was too strong and too incensed to be removed.

Irisa felt her breath leaving her and called on the only thing she could, the darkness, the monstrous, she managed to hiss ‘Forgive me father’ Trying to grasp what she had said, Pero lost his grip very slightly which gave Irisa enough time to pray and call forth the spirits that lay within her, she opened her mouth as the darkness began to spill from it, enveloping itself around Pero, as it took hold and began to burn his skin, he let go of Irisa who fell with a thump onto the hard earth, Francisco grabbed her arms and pulled her away from the writhing Pero.

‘Can you stop it Irisa?’

She wheezed, ‘I am sorry, it is too late.

Within seconds Pero began to scream and as he did so, the air began to stir up all the dust motes, including Pero and he dissolved into the disappearing current, leaving nothing behind.

Servants came running in response to the noise, Irisa sat up, trying to gather her thoughts and her breath.

'Miss what happened? You ok Miss We heard screams!'

'I will be, thank you, I wanted to make sure there were enough herbs to prevent sickness on the ship, stupidly I fell and hit my head on the barrel, must have been me that you heard scream. The priest will look after me now.'

'Yes indeed, thank you young men but I have this now, come Miss Irisa, let us get you back to the house.

Irisa stood and walked slowly with Fransisco, who once out of earshot of the servants, gave a deep sigh. ' I do not know what else we could have done, I am so sorry I could not help you my dear and that you had to protect yourself in that way.'

'It's fine Father, I know you may disagree but at some point Pero was going to either betray one of us or kill one of us, he was so troubled, maybe he'll find peace now. I just worry that this might all be too much for Aleixo. I do not want to jeopardise our plan, I will only tell him if I have to.'

'Today my dear, we are doing what we can to survive, let's get you settled in the house, you must rest for a while.'

Irisa did not trouble to argue, she was totally exhausted and needed to recoup her strength before they began the escape later that evening.

Chapter 40 - Farewells:

Aleixo had been so busy for the most part of the day that he could almost forget what the evening would hold and that from tonight he would no longer be able to hold Irisa at night, they would no longer share their bodies. What would he do if after returning home he could not find a ship that would bring him back to her. Still he tried to take comfort in the fact that he was helping to save three women that night and that had to count for something.

That evening around the table, there was an uneasy silence. There were many toasts to one another, thanks for being such magnanimous hosts, thanks for supporting trade with the 'savages' , thanks for building relationships with the servants and for bringing two wise women to the house that had helped keep the slaves and family well. In short, much patting of one another's backs. Anna and Irisa said little, both constantly going over the plan in their heads of what would happen next, then next etc, each step until they knew it by heart.

The meal finished, the night was dark and the moon was beginning to shine, that night as predicted a blood moon, which had brought many of the servants and slaves out to watch.

'Come my dear Anna. lets' watch this event from the balcony'

'I am sorry, I am so very weary, I am going to retire for the night, but you stay and watch, I know you probably still have matters to discuss with the Captain. '

'As you see fit my dear, goodnight.'

'I wish you all a safe journey home, Irisa. Many thanks for your help whilst you have been with us.'

'Not at all, It has been an honour.'

And so Anna retired, closely followed by Irisa who cited the earlier incident in the stores as a reason for being tired. Aleixo gave an anxious nod but said nothing, so far everything had gone well.

Anna moved swiftly up the stairs, walking straight past her own suite and over to Rosa's closely followed by Irisa. Rosa was already awake, excited by the thought of escaping the island, just like in one of the story books her mother read to her.

Irisa brought out the two caps and the bag of servants' clothes. 'Now these are clean but they will feel rough after being used to fine linens and cottons but it is only for the first few days. She helped Rosa first, who twirled around admiring herself in the small mirror in her bedroom. Then carefully, Irisa pinned all of Rosa's beautiful hair up and affixed the cotton and hair wig onto her head. Rosa giggled and kept touching the African hair with her finger tips. 'Oh mama, it feels so curly and soft.'

Anna laughed and kissed her daughter on the cheek, 'yes, it isn't it, but don't keep touching it, we don't want it to move or God forbid fall off.'

Irsa held Rosa's hands, 'Now little one you are not going to like this bit but I have a pot here of soot and oil and I will need to rub it into your face neck hands and feet, then we will give you a light cloth shawl and you will be ready'

On the contrary, Rosa, delighted in the experience and giggling loudly, said, 'I look like you Irisa!' Irisa smiled back. She stood back from Rosa, 'Well what do you think Anna? at a distance in the dark, will she do?'

'I do believe it will work Irisa, it is really quite convincing from the other side of the room, as long as we stay away from the others, I think we'll fool them.

It took another hour to disguise Anna and gather anything else they might need, then whilst the men were having another 'last toast' to the voyage, Irisa took Rosa and Anna's hands and guided them around the back of the house, where they met Francisco.

'Well praise God you have done a wonderful job ladies! I think, especially with your shawls up, we will convince everyone of who you are. Now come let us make our way to the ship. I have a pony and trap here, the Governor felt it improper for me to walk. Now Irisa, are you coming with us?'

'No Father, I will be here making sure every distraction is in place, when you get to the ship, Aleixo will be there waiting for you, only allow him to help you onto the ship so he can help hide Anna and Rosa, then he will help you off the ship so you can return to me, once the ship is moving we will begin our own journey.'

'Irisa I can not thank you enough for this kindness, my sister is eager for us to return safely, it would not have even been a thought if it were not for you.'

Irisa smiled, 'Don't be too grateful yet, send thanks to my Gods once you are away, thank me by living a full life and allowing Rosa to do the same. I will think about you both often, safe trip.'

Irisa watched the pony and trap as it sedately made its way around the gardens and down the drive until she could no longer see it but could hear the clip-clop of the pony's feet hitting the compacted earth. She prayed she had made the right decision. Finally the Governor took his leave of Vasconcelos who had been provided with a carriage to the port and watched Bellewater shrink away from the pink haze of the blood moon as he made his way to his beloved ship.

Aleixo, his first mate, was waiting for him on board. 'About time we go home then lad?'

'Oh yes Sir! I never want to see this God forsaken land in this or many lifetimes.'

'Where's your slave then? Upset her already eh! She's a mighty headstrong one!'

'That she is, but she's also tired Sir, so she's in my bunk, probably dreading the trip.' he managed a weak smile and the Captain seemed to accept his answers.

Right then this is it boys! There's a wind ready to take us home! Raise the sails, let's fly on this wind!

Aleixo left the mariners to hoist the sails and ran to his cabin, waiting there were Rosa and Anna, quite convincingly dressed as slaves. Looking very anxious. 'Don't worry ladies, I won't let anything happen to you. I want you to stay dressed as you are for the next few days, until it is too late to turn back, then we'll speak to Vasconcelos, at the end of the day he is a gentleman and an Englishman and I do believe he will be pleased to escort you home, he certainly has no love for your husband. I want you to go to Father Francisco's cabin for the first few nights, I'll bring you food and water and you'll have a pallet to sleep on, it will be less obvious that way. Did the priest get away? Or did he decide to stay on the ship?'

Anna spoke quietly, 'No he left, he helped us on the ship, showed us his cabin and yours and how to move discretely around your Juniper, then he unboarded as planned. I think he will get much from living with those indigenous people. I hope that Irisa does, she has earnt peace has she not? She looked up hopefully towards Aleixo. 'Will you try and return to her when you have seen your mother and sisters settled, try to return to be a family with her?'

'Of course if I am able. I am not sure she wants me there, it is her natural habitat, not mine, she will thrive there I am sure, it is what she wanted.'

'She did, but I also think that it was her way of protecting your little family.'

'You keep mentioning family, but the Algonquins as kind as they are would not be family to

start with, they would have to trust me and I'm not sure they could, not in the way they trust Irisa.'
'No Aleixo, your family, surely you noticed? Her feints, her tiredness, her lack of appetite?'

'What are you saying? Oh god lord no! She is carrying my child!' Aleixo felt his heart drop from his mouth, felt a heavy sickness fall upon him. 'Well, I must tell Vasconcelos to turn back now! I have to speak to her! I have to know for sure.'

'Aleixo, she did this to keep herself and the baby safe, she did not tell me, I just guessed, who knows maybe I am wrong but what I do know is that she has risked her life and the life of her friends to allow us to get away. If you return, our plan will be discovered and I do not know how many of us will be killed or hung, is that really what you want? Go home Aleixo, be safe, let Irisa be herself and if you find on your return that you can not live without her, then return, make it happen, but I beg you please let me get my daughter away safely.'

Aleixo gave a loud sob and collapsed to the floor, Anna gently stroked his head and let him unburden himself, then he wiped his face and went up on deck and continued to guide the mariners out to sea

Chapter 41- Freedom Beckons:

Irisa was hiding at the edge of the forest as planned, Francisco met her there, panting from running so far for so long.

'Father, did they make it safely onto the Juniper?'

'Yes my dear, I wasn't sure I could make it all this way back though, kept thinking I'd hear someone shouting that the Governor's wife was missing!'

"We're safe tonight, they always sleep in their separate living quarters, he won't know until late tomorrow morning that they have gone. I believe that Anna has left him a letter being very full and frank, so he'll also know not to chase her if he wants to keep his dignity. Come now, let us make our way towards the Rappahanock river, I believe that's where we'll find Wyono.'

*****

The cooling breeze wrapped around Irisa's body like a sheet of the finest silk and took the sting out of the heat that had burnt down on the village for the past few days. Irisa had sought refuge by the edge of the cliffs, staring out on the aquamarine sea as it met the line of watery blue sky.

She turned to watch Francisco sitting in his leathers on the floor with a group of small children, all drawing with sticks. She smiled at his kindness which had only grown since they had been living with the Algonquins. One of the children waved to Irisa and she waved in return, smiling at the small mulatto girl whose loose ringlets had started to tumble around her neck in this, her fourth year. She ran giggling to Irisa and asked to be picked up.Irisa held her close, and together they looked out to sea.

'Mamma, is that a ship? Is it pappas' ship?'

'No my little one, that's not Pappa Aleixo's ship, but one day we might see it. Come let's go and collect Uncle Francisco, looks like he might need some fish stew, you and your friends have worn him out.'

'No Mamma, I can't, I promised uncle Wyono I would help him hunt Ptarmigan in the woods, he says he will give me my own bow soon, he says if I am very good he will teach me to catch fish with a spear in the sea!'

'Has he indeed, well off you go then.

Irisa watched her go with pride. As much as her heart ached any time Aleixo was mentioned, she knew she had made the right decision for her and her family as she saw the confident little girl running ahead of her. They were all souls of the sea now.

ACKNOWLEDGEMENTS

I would like to send a heartfelt thank you to the late Mr. Smith, my inspirational high school English teacher, who gave me my love of literature to begin with.

I would also like to thank my friends and family, specifically my wonderful husband Stephen for putting up with me blathering on about my book for the past two years, your faith in me has kept me going. Also to my daughters' partners, who have been inundated with tech questions - I apologise.

I would like to end on a thank you to every single person who wished me well, or good luck during the writing process, it really does keep you going on the dark days.

BIBLIOGRAPHY/ FURTHER READING:

African Guardians, European Slave ships and the changing dynamics of power in the modern Atlantic. Stephanie E. Smallwood. The William and Mary Quarterly, 3rd Series. Vol 64 (2007) PP: 699 - 716. Omohundro Institute of Early American history and culture.

Africans and Slave Marriages in the 18th Century, Rio de Janeiro. Flavito do Santos Gomos. The Americans, Vol. 67 No2. October 2010. PP 153 - 184. Cambridge University Press.

A Journey in Chains. Olaudah Euiano. African History. Library of Congress Classroom Materials. 2021.

Early African Religion - What was the first religion? http://quatr.us. Accessed July 2022.

Female Genitle Cutting and the Slave Trade. Economic development institution. edi.apml.co.uk - accessed July 5th 2021.

Historical perspectives of African Burial, New York

blacks and diaspora. ED: Edna Greene Medford. Harvard University Press. Washing DC. (2009) pp 98,100.

http://pancojams.blogspot.com/2014/09 - accessed July 2021.

Liverpoolmuseums.org.uk/history-of-slavery/middlepassage. accessed July2021.

Queen Nzinga (1583-1663) June 16th 2009. Jessica Snethen. Blackpast.org/global-african-history/middlepassage. accessed June 2021.

PortvitiesBristol.discoverbristol.org.uk/slavery/routes . Accessed July 2021.

Research Insight: Female genital cutting and the slave. Economic development Institution. Edi.apml.co.uk. Accessed July 2021.

Slavery and The Making of America. The slave Experience. Kimberly Sambol-Tosco. Thirteen.org/wnet/slavery/relision/history.html.

Slave ships and their crews. The hannibal: en.wikipedia.org. Accessed July 2021.

The reasons for FGM: culture and Tradition. Womens Health News. 91998) March. PMid 12222527

The sons of Neptune and the sons of Ham: A history of Slave ship sailors. E.L. Christopher (2002) https://11Rdiscovery.ucl.ac.uk.

Traditional medicine. Hunawi.com. accessed July 2022.

The Roots of Healing. Archeological and historical investigations of African American Medicine. Erin Brooke Hanbury. (2004) University of Tennessee, Knoxville.

Women Leaders in African History. Ana Nzinga, Queen of Ndongo. In the Heilbrunn Timeline of art history. New York. The Metropolitan Museum of art history. (2002) http://www.metmuseum.org/toah/hd/pwmn.